WRITING FOR THE WEB 3.0

Crawford Kilian

Self-Counsel Press
(a division of)
International Self-Counsel Press Ltd.
USA   Canada

Self-Counsel Press acknowledges the financial support of the Government of Canada through the Book Publishing Industry Development Program (BPIDP) for our publishing activities.

Printed in Canada.

First edition: 1999; 2000
Second edition: 2000
Third edition: 2007

Library and Archives Canada Cataloguing in Publication

Kilian, Crawford, 1941–
    Writing for the web 3.0 / Crawford Kilian. — 3rd ed.

(Self-counsel writing series)
ISBN-13: 978-1-55180-738-6
ISBN-10: 1-55180-738-6

    1. World Wide Web. 2. English language—Rhetoric—Data processing. 3. Web sites—Design. I. Title. II. Series.
TK5105.888.K365 2006   808'.066005   C2006-904842-8

Permissions

The author gratefully acknowledges that the following have generously given permission to reproduce their materials, in whole or in part, in this book:

    In Chapter 5, reference to materials in *Prioritizing Web Usability* (Berkeley: New Riders, 2006), by Jakob Nielsen and Hoa Loranger.

    In Chapter 6, personal quotations from correspondence with Marijke Rijsberman and Stephen Martin.

Self-Counsel Press Ltd.
(a division of)
International Self-Counsel Press Ltd.

1704 North State Street	1481 Charlotte Road
Bellingham, WA 98225	North Vancouver, BC V7J 1H1
USA	Canada

This book is dedicated to all those friends and colleagues
who participated in creating it, and to everyone
who helps to create the Web by writing for it.

CONTENTS

AFTERWORD

APPENDIXES

GLOSSARY

EXERCISES

PREFACE

or almost 40 years I've taught workplace writing, freelance article writing, and how to write commercial fiction. This is my 20th book. So I'm pretty dedicated to print on paper as a medium of communication.

But in the late 1980s I began to see how networked computers were changing the way we communicate. In some ways they were just another means of getting print on paper, but something about the medium was changing the nature of our messages — and changing the nature of our relationship to the people we communicated with. First in email, and then on the World Wide Web, we were reading, writing, and reacting to information in different ways.

In teaching technology students in the early 1990s, I had to learn fast to stay ahead of them. We were all scrambling to master the new grammar of multimedia: the ways that text and sound and image could combine to express ideas. With few authorities to turn to, my students and I watched what we ourselves were doing, and we tried to draw general principles from our experience.

By the mid-1990s the Web was truly worldwide, and a whole new industry arose to serve and advance it. I got a sense of how big it was when I walked into a university bookstore and found, by rough estimate, 170 shelf-feet of books about the Web: how to master HTML, CGI, and Java; how to use this or that browser; how to design websites; how to research the exponentially growing resources available on the Web.

Not one of those books dealt with the actual words to be used on the Web.

Well, that made a certain amount of sense. No one had enough experience yet to say just what would work on the Web and what wouldn't. Hypertext had been around in various forms since the 1970s, but it wouldn't necessarily work on the Web the way it does in, for example, an encyclopedia CD-ROM. So most of the Web pioneers wrote in whatever style seemed comfortable, and other pioneers followed their lead. That's why, in the late 1990s, so many sites had expressions like "Check it out" and "This site under construction."

By then, creating websites had changed from a self-taught skill into an industry. The pioneers had given countless hours to trial and error, mostly error, in learning the basics of a new technology. But they couldn't squander their time when clients were paying for it. An obscure computer specialty in 1992 had become almost a basic job skill by the end of the decade. My own colleagues, teaching in fields such as tourism and business administration, began to wonder how they could cram website design into an already crowded curriculum. If they couldn't, their graduates risked losing out to skilled competitors.

So the time seemed right for a book that might help both expert and novice webwriters save time and avoid known pitfalls. It might thereby help Web users as well.

No doubt this book reflects my own biases toward print on paper, but I have tried to learn from a wide range of self-taught pioneer Web authorities and to present their views as well as my own. If my arguments make sense and help you write successful text for your sites, of course I'll be delighted. But I look forward to being rebutted and superseded, because better insights will make the Web a more effective communication tool for all of us. Some of my arguments may provoke you into articulating contrary views that work to make your sites succeed. If so, this book has succeeded too.

In mastering writing for the Web, we learn about what goes on in other kinds of writing as well, and what goes on in our own minds. So in learning how to write well for this medium, I think we learn how to write better in all media, and we learn something about ourselves too.

ACKNOWLEDGMENTS

As I look back on the creation of this book through three editions, I can see it's been a highly interactive process. Many people responded to versions or excerpts from it, making me reconsider my earlier views.

I thank the online colleagues who graciously permitted me to quote from their email correspondence, websites, and published books: Robert E. Horn, Stephen Martin, Jakob Nielsen, Debbie Ridpath Ohi, Gareth Rees, and Marijke Rijsberman. A special thank-you to Steve Outing and Amy Gahran, whose Online Writers list and late lamented Content Exchange provided lively forums for discussion of the online medium.

My own students in Canada and Brazil have contributed greatly to my understanding of online writing, and I should thank those in particular who prodded me to make myself clearer as I taught (and learned) the principles of hypertext writing: Bev Chiu, Besire Culhaoglu, Luis Filidis, Kelly Gomes, David Ingram, Raj Kamal, Sarah King, Rhona MacInnes, Adrian McInnes, Ross McKerlich, Sandy Meyer, Michelle Morelos, Deirdre Radomske, Mercedes Sanchez, Gabriela Schonbach, and Michael Souvage.

I also thank Judy Phillips, who edited the first edition of *Writing for the Web*; Richard Day, who edited the second; and Barbara Kuhne, who edited this third version.

INTRODUCTION

After 15 years with the Web, most people don't know how they ever got along without it. Yet old habits die hard, and we still use the web with habits acquired in other media.

So newspaper websites still look for the most part like newspapers. TV station websites offer lots of video. Businesses' websites look like their ads in the Yellow Pages, only with more colors. And most website creators treat it like whatever medium they're most familiar with: a sheet of typing paper, a radio, a canvas, a family photo album, or a Rolodex.

Websites can serve all those functions, but one of their primary purposes is to make large amounts of text available online. (The Latin word for "web," by the way, is *textus*.) Graphics and sound can enhance the content of a site, but text remains the core.

The Web is a very different medium from print, TV, and radio. But the habits we've learned in those media influence the way we respond to text on the computer screen. We even call web files "pages" when they're nothing of the sort.

We read print documents in a certain way, using cues to navigate through a familiar format. The indented first line of a paragraph tells us a new topic is coming up. Page numbers establish a sequence we're happy to follow. Indexes use alphabetical order to help us find things. We're so used to these conventions that we don't even notice them.

But print habits don't apply on the Web. We surf through TV channels with our remote control, and we bring the same attitude to the TV-like screen of our computer: deliver something interesting *right now*, some kind of jolt or reward, or we'll go somewhere else.

These responses demand a kind of writing that is different from other media — not better or worse, just different. Effective website creation can certainly include excellent video, graphics, and sound, but it also means text that will halt impatient surfers and make them read what you've written.

This book offers some principles for composing text for your website. The principles aren't carved in stone (how could they be?), but they arise from the experience of thousands of people writing online and on the Web over the past 20 years. We can draw some general conclusions about what works and what doesn't. We can also modify or ignore those conclusions if our own circumstances require it. When George Orwell compiled his list of rules for clear writing, he saved the best for last: "Break any of these rules sooner than say anything outright barbarous."

Good webtext has a lot in common with good print text. It's plain, concise, concrete, and "transparent": even on a personal blog, the text shouldn't draw attention to itself, only to its subject. This book will give you plenty of exercises and tips for developing such a writing style.

Like good print text, webtext carries a subtext, a nonverbal message. The message may be, "I'm comfortable in this medium and I understand you, my reader." Or it may be, "I'm completely wrapped up in my own ego and my love of cool stuff." This book should help sensitize you to any writing habits that may unconsciously let the wrong subtext slip out.

I can't tell you how to design your site. But I can try to alert you to the likely results of your design decisions. For example, if you like long, long paragraphs full of long, long words, your readers will quickly lose interest in what you have to say. Similarly, if your text scrolls on forever, you will lose readers. If you build your site with layer after layer of linked pages, you will likely baffle and bore your readers.

If you are creating your own commercial site, or a personal blog, you decide the content and the structure: its topics, its size, how its pages connect, how its graphics, text, audio, and video work together. For reasons I'll discuss, you can easily undercut yourself by presenting text as if it were still on paper. So it's in your own interest to understand something about website design basics, especially as they affect the display of text.

If you're writing text for a site designed by someone else, you face other constraints. The site designers may not have known or cared about the kind of text displays you need. Navigation aids may not be good enough. All too often, such sites are designed by techies who go with what looks cool, not with what users need. Or a senior manager with no knowledge of the Web may have the final word on both design and content.

If you're working on a corporate website, how to write good text is only one of your challenges. You may need to explain some basics about the medium to your colleagues — and again, while I don't deal directly with design issues, you'll need to understand some realities about the medium if you're going to use it effectively. And whether you're writing for a small personal blog or a big corporate website, effectiveness is the whole point of your effort.

So let's start at the beginning, with what makes your computer screen a different medium from this printed page.

Computers condition us for "high joltage." A jolt is an emotional reward that follows a prescribed action. Turn on the TV at the right time for your favorite program, and it delivers jolts. Watch a movie and it delivers jolts. Log on to your favorite forum or chat room, and you get jolts of praise or blame.

Like Pavlov's dogs, computer users are now conditioned to expect such stimuli. Maybe it's a jolt of surprise as our computer beeps or boings. Maybe it's a jolt of triumph as we find information we've been hunting for. Or a jolt of satisfaction when someone has linked to our blog because we've posted something good.

Yes, it's a kind of addiction. We feel deprived if we don't get some kind of jolt at regular intervals, so we go where we hope to find more jolts — to websites.

Does this mean your own site needs to look and sound like a rock video? Or that you need to use obscene language to get and keep your visitors' attention? Not at all.

A truly high-joltage website supplies the information its visitors are looking for. But your text had better be invitingly brief, and it should provide the simple jolt of being under-standable in one quick glance.

If it also intrigues your visitors by offering a hook of some kind so they'll keep reading, so much the better. Your role as a webwriter is to make your reader's job effortless.

To sum up: By combining text, graphics, video, and audio, the Web offers some of the qualities of familiar media like print, TV, movies, and radio. When we recognize those qualities, we respond as if we were dealing with print or TV or radio. As a writer, you should understand this mindset and compose your text accordingly.

You should also accept the strengths and the weaknesses of the Web. Your readers may want to treat your site like a book or magazine or TV show, but it's still a website — a collection of electronic files that you may organize as you see fit, but that your readers will explore in any sequence they like. That puts you in an interesting bind: your readers will read the material as text, and you may think of it as text, but it's really hypertext. (In Chapter 1 we'll look at what that means for you as a webwriter.)

This edition of *Writing for the Web* is also a kind of hypertext. It comes with a CD containing a number of additional resources, including a PowerPoint slide show and a great many links. These include all the sites mentioned in the text, plus many related sites also worth exploring. In addition, my blog Writing for the Web (http://crofsblogs.typepad.com) will offer continuous updates of those links. I'll also add whatever new materials I find — and that you let me know about. This is, after all, an interactive medium.

Note: My editors and I have made every effort to verify the accuracy of URLs in this book (and its CD) as of publication date. However, since website addresses are constantly changing, not every cited URL may be accessible. If you find a particular URL doesn't lead to the indicated site, a search engine may help find the site's new or alternative location.

Whenever possible, I will post revised URLs on the book's blog, Writing for the Web (http://crofsblogs.typepad.com).

1

HISTORY, HYPERTEXT, AND INTERACTIVE COMMUNICATION

As World War II was nearing its end, an American scientist named Vannevar Bush published an article that now looks highly prophetic. "As We May Think" (www.theatlantic.com/doc/194507/bush) argued the urgent need to make knowledge far more accessible.

As director of the wartime Office of Scientific Research and Development, Bush understood very well that information had become almost unmanageable. The atomic bomb was a top-secret project fully known to only a few hundred scientists. Yet even the bomb had generated a white-water flood of information. Government, business, science — every field was generating so much information that no one could follow it.

Computers in Bush's day were huge and crude, but microfilm was beginning to put whole bookshelves' worth of information onto small reels of celluloid. A little electric motor could zip you through many weeks' worth of newspaper pages, or through the pages of a long technical report — all projected onto a small screen. Bush dreamed of a camera that would take pictures of specific pages, so you could revisit them whenever you chose.

Microfilm never fulfilled Bush's dreams, but as recently as the 1970s, microfiche looked like a serious step forward: a hundred pages of text on a sheet of film the size of a postcard!

As a young technical writer in the mid-1960s, I saw the scientists at the Lawrence Berkeley Laboratory struggling to keep up with "the literature" — the articles published in their particular specialties. By then computers were less crude, but they could still fill a large room. Primitive databases on huge reels of magnetic tape were being used — databases that tried to organize the ever-increasing flood of information. Some of the lab's tech writers were using them to help scientists refine their searches, but it was a slow and painful process. The tech writers didn't know it, but they were trying to create Google.

At almost exactly the same time, a young computer genius named Ted Nelson launched Project Xanadu (www .xanadu.com), an attempt to realize Vannevar Bush's dream using something Nelson called *hypertext*. It wasn't (and isn't) what we now call hypertext. Nelson's "deep hypertext" model called for two-way links and quotations that would always be linked to their original sources. On the home page of Project Xanadu, the World Wide Web is dismissed as "another imitation of paper [that] trivializes our original hypertext model."

Perhaps it does. But the Web is what we're now stuck with, and hypertext is the term we use to describe how we use the Web: a way of connecting text, graphics, video, and audio that uses computers to realize the dream of Vannevar Bush.

Is it Web or web?

Technically, *World Wide Web* is a proper noun, usually shortened to *Web*. But the weight of usage in the last few years has been to use lowercase except when referring to the Web as a system of linked sites and pages. So in this book I'll use lowercase *w* (*webwriting, website*) except when referring to the Web itself.

1. Plain Text Versus Hypertext

If you want to learn about, say, vampires, you face a pretty tedious process if you plan to research the topic using a multivolume encyclopedia. Perhaps you would first go to the volume with all the *V* entries to find *Vampires*. That entry may then suggest you also look at entries in other volumes: Transylvania; Dracula; Stoker, Bram; Lugosi, Bela; films, horror; bats, vampire; films, German: Nosferatu. As you consult each of these entries, you're pulling heavy volumes off the shelf and replacing them, making notes, and generally taking up a lot of time.

Even using a single-volume book to research a topic presents challenges. Such a book may have its own hypertext — cross-references and references to external sources of information — in the form of footnotes, endnotes, appendixes, bibliographies, and an index — even scribbles in the margin by the last reader. The researcher looking for particular information soon learns to read starting with the index and then jumping to pages dealing with the subject of interest. Even then, the follow-up work of tracking down footnoted references and finding titles mentioned in the bibliography can be tedious and frustrating.

The theory is that hypertext saves you much of that work. Each hypertext document has electronic links to other hypertext documents, much like doors between rooms in a library. If you're reading a hypertext document about horror films and you find mention of Bela Lugosi, the actor's name can itself be a link to still more information. Instead of making notes, you can simply save the file about Lugosi along with all the other items you've encountered.

And if you don't want to read about Bela Lugosi, but you do want to read about vampire bats or Transylvanian history, you can ignore the link to the Hollywood star and continue on with your reading.

This freedom of choice has its attractions, but some hyper-text pioneers have tried to make it look like a revolution on a Gutenbergian scale. They claim that, freed from the tyranny of the author's structure, readers can now examine any document they like, in any order they choose, and use the information any way they please. (Of course, readers can also read a printed document any way they please, but it takes more effort to jump back and forth in a paper document than in an electronic document.)

If many items of information are small, maybe just a para-graph or even a sentence, then readers probably have numerous links to follow. Instead of being led like children by the author's hand, readers can make the text their own property, linking its components in their own preferred way.

Having all this choice is not always useful, however. If we just want to find out about Bram Stoker, we don't want to waste time linking to a site on Bela Lugosi, even if the author thinks Lugosi is important.

But most of the time, as readers, we expect the author to have mapped out our route for us, just as we expect a travel agent to plan details of our trip. We assume the travel agent knows more than we do and can anticipate our needs. Maybe we want some options built into our itinerary, but we generally don't want to fly from New York to Paris, back to New York, and then to Frankfurt.

Pushed to a logical extreme, the hypertext author might as well hand the reader a set of Scrabble tiles and say: "Here, make your own text." But that's not authorship, any more than 52 Pickup is a card game. Our readers expect some kind of coherence in our hypertext. We can and should provide such coherence, but we should be aware of some specific challenges in doing so.

Hypertext is by definition nonlinear, but remember that *linearity* itself is just a metaphor for a one-at-a-time sequence — especially a sequence we're familiar with. The sequence A-B-C is linear insofar as that's the sequence we have learned. So is 1-2-3, and so is subject-verb-object. Because we've memorized certain patterns, we can expect D to follow C, 3 to follow 2, and verb (usually) to follow subject.

When we put information into a numbered sequence, for example, we expect #1 to be more important or more basic than #2. That's because we're used to hearing important or introductory material before we hear details or complicated material that assumes we understand the basics.

What is hypertext, anyway?

An essay or paper with footnotes or a bibliography is a kind of hypertext since it leads you to another portion of the text, or to other documents in a way that makes it fairly easy to find them. A document with annotations in the margins could also be considered hypertext. But in this book, *hypertext* will be used to refer to linked documents in electronic format containing text, graphics, audio, video, or some combination of these elements.

The links enable readers to jump between documents —
even if the documents are on remote computers far away
from one another.

2. The Interactive Communication Model

In the rest of this book, I'll examine some of the problems —
and opportunities — that hypertext offers to you as a webwriter. But you should also bear in mind that hypertext
depends on a completely different kind of communication
model than print, film, TV, and radio: the online medium is
interactive, and that makes a huge difference in what you say
and the way you say it. It even creates a different culture than
that of earlier media.

The standard model, also called the instrumentalist model,
treats a message like a FedEx package. All the recipient has to
do is sign for it: buy the product, vote for the candidate, give
the right answer on the exam. In the interactive model (also
called the constructivist model), both sides are creating a conversation. They are construing the meaning of that conversation by learning more about each other.

The unspoken message in the standard model is, "Do what
I say." In the interactive model, the unspoken message is, "Is
this what you want?"

As we will see, many corporate websites (both business and
government) still operate on the standard model. Their sponsors see your computer screen as just another spot where they
can slap up a copy of their one-way message. Good webwriting,
though, should exploit this opportunity for a two-way conversation — whatever the purpose and content of your site.

As I've watched the interactive culture emerge online since
the 1980s, I've seen key traits emerge. Standard culture wants

to know the right answers; interactive culture wants to know the right questions. Standard culture likes to learn from success; interactives learn more from failures and mistakes. Standard culture looks to the future; interactive culture demands immediate results.

Interactives tend to be egalitarian, respecting other people not for their social status or rank, but for their expertise and willingness to share knowledge. Standard culture adherents wait for someone to give the order; interactives decide what to do and then do it.

I'm not suggesting that interactive culture is somehow better than standard culture — it's just different, and it's different because of the technology the interactive model emerges from. That technology gives you, as a webwriter, both limits and opportunities. As you develop content for your website, you should bear in mind some basic facts about the medium and its users.

3. Computers Make Us Impatient

We used to call it the World Wide Wait, because the primitive dial-up systems of the 1990s were so slow to load pages. Many users in those days would set their browsers to ignore the graphics, since these are always the slowest items to load.

That impatience is still with us. But now we're impatient to get right to the material we came looking for, and we're likely to hit the Back button if the page doesn't come up right that instant.

4. Computers Give Us Jolts

When you're operating a car, it responds immediately to your actions. Ideally, so do computers. Hit the right combination of keys and you get music, or a window opens, or email pops up.

Text itself can elicit immediate responses in us and give us jolts — anything from seeing our name on someone else's site, to reading a message from an old friend, to finding a scrap of information we've been searching for.

A "high-joltage" website will attract and hold more visitors than one providing few stimuli. This doesn't mean you should write in a hysterical style; it means writing clear text with your readers in mind.

5. Computer-Screen Text Is Hard to Read

You may not realize it, but your monitor has very low resolution. Maybe the text looks crisp and sharp compared to that on the old green-on-black monitors of the mid-1980s, but take a long look at your text onscreen and then at a laser printout. The printed text will be a sight for sore eyes, and you'll realize how difficult it is to read lots of text onscreen.

Studies in the 1980s, reported by Web analyst and usability advocate Jakob Nielsen, found that reading from a monitor was 25 percent slower than reading print on paper. This seemed to result from the poor resolution of computer screens. In 1998, Nielsen was reporting that expensive experimental monitors with very high resolution could bring reading speeds back up to normal. He predicted high-end users would have such screens by 2003, and all users by 2008. Then in his 2006 book *Prioritizing Web Usability*, he was predicting that most of us would have medium-size, high-resolution screens by 2009.

But many computer users will be stuck with small, low-resolution screens for the foreseeable future. Even those of us with high-resolution screens still find long pieces of text hard to read. For many impatient, jolt-hungry readers, this is a problem: They simply won't stick around to read long text.

Reading from a monitor is tiring in other ways as well: try reading this book while holding it straight out in front of you at arm's length. When your arms get tired, just prop it up at the same distance. It feels unnatural because it *is* unnatural. You'd rather hold the book in your lap, or on a tabletop within one foot of your eyes.

To improve the readability of your text, you could provide lots of blank space around it, as you would in a résumé. This means limiting the amount of text you put on a single screen.

You may choose to display your text in a column that reaches only halfway across the screen, leaving wide margins on either side or areas of blank space that provide respite for your readers' eyes. While this display may mean that readers will have to scroll down the page to read the full article, shortening the length of the lines makes text more readable. This is why newspapers display text in narrow columns.

Jakob Nielsen and others have found that the longer we read text on a screen, the worse our ability to spot mistakes. All kinds of errors and typos escape correction — especially in boldface headings and subheads. This means onscreen text is hard to proofread. Our visitors, however, are likely to spot our mistakes very quickly.

6. Websites Attract Different Kinds of Visitors

We often change roles as we use the Web. It's useful to think about those roles and how they influence the way we respond to online text.

Lookers and **listeners** are most interested in graphics and sound. Text doesn't really interest them except as a guide to the next video clip, graphic image, song, or podcast. **Listeners** may also include persons with visual impairments who need text that's understandable when spoken by a voice program.

Users are looking for information. They include customers as well as researchers. They like "chunks" — stand-alone blocks of information, filling the screen with 100 words or less, requiring little or no scrolling. Users need concise, well-organized, and well-mapped sites so they can go straight to what they want.

Readers want information too, but they are willing to scroll through complete documents. They may well prefer text adapted for screen display. Better yet, they like printer-friendly versions that they can print out and read on paper.

Talkers are visitors who want to comment on what they find on your site, and perhaps create a link to it on their own sites — especially if they're running web logs (blogs) dealing with the same subjects you also deal with. (Thanks to my Brazilian student Luis Filidis for this insight.)

Colleagues may obtain your information through an intranet accessible only to employees. Such visitors need clear, usable, well-formatted information just as much as outsiders do.

Customers want to buy something from you. They certainly want information, but they also want clear, simple steps that let them buy what they want.

Depending on the nature of your site, you should try to appeal to as many different kinds of visitors as possible. If you're a graphic designer looking for work, for example, your site should feature many examples of your work — and also plenty of text describing your background, skills, and philosophy.

Bear in mind also that your visitors may not be native speakers of your language, or very highly educated. Your text needs to be understandable and usable to them as well.

7. Webtext Is Hypertext

Your visitors can jump around from one page to another in any sequence they like. This means that the content of every page should be able to stand on its own, without reference to other documents except through clear links. As a webwriter you must be able to create such stand-alone documents and make it easy for your visitors to jump to other documents on your site (or on other sites).

Given the nature of this medium, and the interactive, international culture it has encouraged, writing for the Web is often very different from writing for print on paper. But it is a skill well worth mastering.

2

STRUCTURING YOUR WEBSITE

A s a website author, you should be mentally organizing your material; your readers need not be aware of any structure or organization, but if you visualize some kind of pattern for your material, it will at least make your own writing easier. If you understand reader behavior and the built-in problems of navigation, you can minimize the effects of these problems. Throwing information into your website at random will only make it chaotic.

One web page of hypertext can be any length, from a single letter or numeral to the collected works of Tolstoy. But for ease of reading, a computer monitor should normally display the equivalent of only one-third to one-half of a page of double-spaced typescript — say about 100 words. You can, of course, pack much more than that into a single screen that you do not scroll, but only if you reduce the point size of your type to illegibility and single-space the text. This is sure to drive your readers away: the eye recoils from unbroken masses of text, whether on a printed page or a computer screen.

You have two choices for organizing your material: to chunk it or scroll it. That is, display it in one screenful of 100 words or less, or in a long strip of text that the reader must scroll through.

Your choice will depend on the material itself and how your readers are likely to use it. The Web is good for two kinds of information retrieval: hit-and-run, and downloading.

1. Chunking: Hit-and-Run Information Retrieval

Hit-and-run information retrieval is what most of us do when we surf the Web. We visit a site, see if anything looks interesting, click around, get our jolt (or fail to get it), and go on to another site. Maybe we found nothing much or maybe the site changed our lives. As webwriters we should notice that the information we retrieved was probably contained on one screen. The author had to present it as briefly and dramatically as possible so it would hold our attention and be easy to understand, and perhaps lead us to go on to other small chunks of information within the site. (Many webwriters use the word *chunk* to describe whatever information you can fit on a single screen; we'll use the term in this way also.)

When chunking, you break your material up into segments of not much more than 100 words (often much less), so that every word within a chunk is visible on a monitor. This helps the reader to grasp all the information on the page. Two or more chunks, when linked electronically, form a *stack*. Links will take readers to other pages in the stack, often by several different pathways.

A chunk may include more than one paragraph, and may also include headings, subheads, and graphics — even links to video and audio. It often helps to display chunked text double-spaced for easier reading.

However, some visitors are reluctant to explore another page in the hypertext stack. You'd better make sure the first page readers encounter provides plenty of reasons for them to explore deeper into your stack. I'll discuss ways to do so in the next chapter. I'll also discuss ways to organize chunked text into clear hierarchies.

Sound and pictures can undercut text

In the early days of television commercials, advertisers discovered to their horror that they were actually sabotaging themselves by using images so fantastic that viewers were distracted from the products being advertised. They knew that viewers wanted jolts in the form of vivid and dramatic images, even if they were in black and white, and they knew they had to outdo their competitors, who were also trying to stop viewers from heading for the bathroom during the commercial breaks. So advertising was filled with wild and wonderful images that would command attention.

But when advertisers conducted follow-up interviews and market research, they learned that consumers rarely connected the fantastic images on the screen with the products that the images were supposed to help sell. The images were actually making people tune out the message.

Rosser Reeves, a 1950s advertising guru, called this effect "vampire video." Once he had understood and named the problem, his commercials didn't abandon vivid graphics, but the images became strictly subordinate to the message. Sometimes they were even the message itself: if viewers turned off the sound, they still got the sales pitch delivered as onscreen text.

Reeves's ads passed the critical test: people got the message and bought the product.

The Web is now in a stage comparable to 1950s television advertising and 1980s computer design. In the mid-1980s, computers began to offer simple graphics and a choice of fonts. People produced cluttered, ugly documents with several fonts per page, plus Dingbats and clip art. Website creators are still doing awful things with graphics and audio, partly because they can and partly because they don't yet know they shouldn't.

Your choices as a web author will depend on the relative importance of text and graphics for the website you are creating. If you're a graphic artist displaying your work, your text will be minimal, even nonexistent.

If text is critical, then bells and whistles should appear only when they enhance the message (that is, make it more understandable, more surprising, more persuasive) or make the text more interesting.

2. Scrolling: Long Documents, PDFs, and Downloading

Sometimes readers surf online for very detailed information — perhaps a government report or a long news story, or maybe even a whole book. It would be pointless to break up such texts into independent chunks to be read in any order; the original authors intended them to be read in a certain sequence, with all the usual navigation cues of linear text printed on paper. In any case, the text may be too long to fit on the screen all at once, so the reader will end up scrolling through such documents.

Long, linear-text documents really belong on paper, however. A website acts as an archive for making them available for downloading. You don't need to worry quite as much about brevity with these documents; readers who want to scrutinize them can download them to their hard drives and then print them out in whatever format they prefer.

However, many visitors who are downloading documents from your website will read at least part of such a document on the monitor, whatever the cost in slowed reading speed and eyestrain. This is often true of PDF files. Scrolling tires out most readers very quickly, so it is a good idea to at least provide some internal links, such as a list of keyword links at the top of the file. (If you have Adobe Acrobat, you can create internal links when you create a PDF document — and you can also create links in the PDF to other websites and to other online documents.)

Clicking on an internal link will take readers directly to the section of interest, enabling them to rappel like rock climbers down the text. When they are finished reading a particular section, they can jump back to the top to find something else. A list of keywords also provides a useful overview of the text's main parts. For details on navigation, see Chapter 3.

If you expect most visitors to download the archived text and print it out, then don't worry about its online readability. If you are providing a document as a PDF, of course you can keep the format of the original document. That could be ordinary single- or double-spaced word-processed text, or it could be an elaborately designed report with color photos and other graphics. (However, keep in mind that most readers do not have color printers.)

If you do expect visitors to read your text online, it would be a good idea to alter the formatting a little bit. Single-space your documents, with a double space between paragraphs. That makes paragraph indentations unnecessary, and gives your readers a welcome patch of white space between paragraphs to make reading easier. Without such breaks, readers get lost in a mass of text.

When deciding whether to chunk or scroll your text, you're not facing a clear-cut decision between a "bad" design (long, scrolling text) and a "good" one (chunks of text): both have their uses. As a writer, you must decide whether your material is more useful in chunks written for hit-and-run readers, or in scrolling text meant to be printed out on paper. Whether you're writing for the hit-and-run reader or the downloader, you should be presenting text that's as clear, brief, and useful as you can make it.

Displaying long text on a blog

On many blogs, the author simply displays long posts as scrolling text on the site's front page. This creates an additional problem: If the blog displays just one long scrolling text, readers may not want to scroll down to see what else is on the page.

One solution, available through programs such as TypePad, is to break the long post in two: headline plus a few lines on the front page, with a link to a new page where the whole text is available. This allows visitors to go through the whole text only if they wish to, and makes it easier for them to scan the front page for other posts and links.

You can also make long posts easier to read with a few simple adjustments to the layout of the text. If you display your text in a column about one-half to one-third the width of your screen, each line will be only about 10 or 12 words long. Most people find this to be a comfortable line length to read, although, of course, it means still more scrolling.

3. The Three Principles of Webtext

You may intend your website to be simply an electronic archive of writing designed to be text on paper. Or you may be using hypertext in avant-garde literary experiments for small audiences. In such cases, you can happily ignore the advice that follows. Otherwise, whatever the purpose and content of your site, I suggest that your text reflect three basic principles: Orientation, Information, and Action.

Let's look at a couple of examples in which the same principles apply with text on paper. In a business letter, for example, you supply appropriate background information and use standard formatting (Orientation) to help the reader make sense of your main message (Information) and to understand what should happen as a result of that information (Action). Another example is an advertisement with your logo in which you explain that overcrowding in your warehouse is forcing you to offer widgets at unheard-of low prices, and customers can act on that information by calling your toll-free telephone number.

These principles operate very similarly in webtext.

3.1 Orientation: Where am I and how do I get around this site?

When visitors arrive at your site, they need two kinds of orientation: background knowledge about the site, and navigation aids to help them get around the site. So the front page of your site should orient your readers by telling them —

- what the site is about,

- how it is organized, and

- how to navigate it.

Sometimes the title of the site tells visitors what it's about:

Your Guide to Chesterton

Often, however, you may need a few lines of explanation (sometimes known as a subtitle or catchphrase):

The complete directory of Chesterton's tourist attractions, businesses, and municipal services.

You may also need to elaborate on your organizational principle:

This site consists of six main pages: <u>Tourist Attractions</u>, <u>Lodging</u>, <u>Dining</u>, <u>Business Guide</u>, <u>Municipal Services</u>, and <u>Community News</u>.

Or you may present these topics as a set of buttons or graphics. You may want to offer more direct links from the front page by making it look like a table of contents:

<u>Municipal Services</u>

   <u>City Hall</u>

   <u>Police</u>

   <u>Parks Department</u>

   <u>School Board</u>

   <u>Highways Office</u>

   <u>Hospital</u>

I discuss navigation cues such as a table of contents and navigation buttons in more detail in Chapter 3.

In judging the effectiveness of your orientation, you can apply two secondary principles: minimalism and coherence.

3.1a Minimalism

Is the orientation you are supplying more than the reader needs? If you're tempted to begin an orienting statement with, "As you probably know," you can probably drop the statement altogether. Minimalism also means you shouldn't put too many items of information on your site. Every item may potentially add to the reader's navigation problems, so be sure that each one has a good reason for being there. Sometimes a link to another site is all you need.

3.1b Coherence

Does a given chunk of text make sense on its own? If it deals with two or three ideas in 100 words or so, do you supply clear transitions from one idea to the next? Does this chunk behave like other chunks on your site? For example, suppose you have a chunk describing a local hotel, with links to nearby restaurants; will other "lodging" chunks also link in the same way to restaurants? Once your readers understand your navigation system, they will expect to use it throughout your site, so endeavor to be consistent.

Don't forget that since many readers may first come to your site through a page other than your front page, orientation is important on every single page of your website. But it need not always be quite as detailed as on your front page.

3.2 Information: The reason for the site's existence

Your site provides readers with information in the form of text and graphics, whether displayed on several linked pages or on one long, scrolling page. Whatever that information may include, two secondary principles are at work here: clarity and correctness.

3.2a Clarity

Your text should be understandable at first glance, even to readers with little formal education or from a different cultural background. If readers must puzzle over unfamiliar or ambiguous words, you are making them work harder than they need to.

This is true even if your site deals with a specialized topic. For example, suppose you have created a site with highly technical information about extensible markup language (XML), which is a way of writing code for websites. Are you using long, complicated words just because you can, when shorter ones would really be more clear and straightforward? Even your expert readers deserve the simplest, clearest information you can provide.

3.2b Correctness

On one level, correctness means basics such as proper spelling, good grammar, and accurate names and addresses. This kind of correctness is also part of clarity because it helps readers understand your message more easily.

But every message has two components, verbal and nonverbal, and if they are in conflict, readers tend to trust the nonverbal *subtext* message. For example, spelling or grammatical errors on a lawyer's website create a subtext about the lawyer's poor attention to detail. Any professional or business website must convey a subtext message of competence; errors in language basics and errors of fact undercut that message.

3.3 Action: What people can do once they are informed

What action do you want your readers to take as a result of absorbing the information on your website? Should they email you, provide a credit card number, subscribe to a newsletter, or click on the link to your advertisers? If you are going to get the results you want, you need to consider two secondary principles: a positive attitude and the "you" attitude.

3.3a A positive attitude

Regardless of the content of your website, write the text with a positive slant. Even if your site is denouncing violations of human rights or the destruction of the environment, you must think your users can do something about those problems. Otherwise, why bother to create a site? So, when you present problems, suggested solutions should be close at hand: documents with important information, links to groups with political influence, or email addresses of powerful people.

A positive attitude is easier to express if you avoid negative expressions altogether. Consider the positive wording in the right-hand column below:

You won't be disappointed.	You're sure to be pleased.
Please don't hesitate to email us.	Please email us.

3.3b The "you" attitude

Webwriting should present facts and ideas in terms of how they will serve readers. So be sure to talk more about your readers than about yourself. Instead of writing —

I've listed the top 15 companies I consider a threat to the environment.

you can write:

You can email your protests to the top 15 environmental polluters.

This is more than simple courtesy. Your readers have their own purposes for coming to your site, and you are there to serve those purposes. If you understand what your readers want and you anticipate their needs, your site will succeed and your readers will visit your site.

Avoid *egophilia*, the habit of starting sentences with expressions such as "I feel" or "I think." You may think such expressions suggest modesty by reducing a flat assertion to a statement of opinion, but in fact you are injecting yourself into the sentence. Better to stick with the flat assertion.

Instead of writing —

I feel this is the best hiking trail in the park.

write:

This is the best hiking trail in the park.

Instead of —

I believe you'd be wise to take out travel insurance before you leave.

write:

You'd be wise to take out travel insurance before you leave.

An important way of conveying the "you" attitude is by showing consideration for your readers. They are doing you a favor by visiting your site, and you owe them a rewarding experience. Will they really want to scroll through your list of the 100 worst movies of all time? Will they follow one of your links to a File Not Found message? An out-of-date site with "link rot" (links that go nowhere) wastes readers' time.

So put yourself in your readers' shoes: If you were a stranger arriving at your own site, would you feel as if the site's creator had made a special effort to make life easy for you?

If we accept these three principles of webwriting — orientation, information, and action — several useful guidelines for structuring content emerge. The next chapter discusses them in detail.

3

ORGANIZING
WEBSITE
CONTENT

obert E. Horn, in his book *Mapping Hypertext*, points out that linear text is full of cues that help the reader navigate. For example, print text is generally organized hierarchically. We expect each section to include a general statement or thesis, supported by various kinds of evidence or illustration. We start a book with an overview or introduction that summarizes important points, and we often find that chapters of the book feature similar introductions.

In hypertext, says Horn, we need to present the whole hierarchy of the text in some kind of overview, such as a navigation bar whose buttons will take us to different sections within the text. Let's begin our discussion of organizing website content by looking at navigation cues.

1. Orientation: Navigation Cues Provide a Site Overview

Your front page may include a big headline and a summary about the purpose of the site, but it should essentially be a table of contents. You can organize your hypertext in a number of ways, including —

- alphabetically,

- numerically,

- chronologically,

- graphically, or

- completely at random (which I don't recommend).

A list of departments within your organization would naturally be alphabetical — probably just a string of letter-links (A, B, C, etc.) across the screen. So would a list of employees' telephone numbers and email addresses. A sequence describing a process in time might be a numbered list; so might a categorical list of topics running from most important to least important.

Many websites use graphical contents pages. These can range from something as simple as an organizational chart to an elaborate map with numerous graphic cues: a cartoon of a police officer in a kiosk, for example, linking to the name and telephone number of the company's security officer.

Be careful when using graphical cues in the place of textual cues. Many new visitors may not recognize the cartoon as a link, which will defeat its purpose.

If you're confident that your graphics are intuitive and self-explanatory to anyone from any cultural or educational background, you don't have to worry about refining the text on your contents page. Otherwise, try to make your text as clear as possible, even if it seems redundant to those who do understand the graphics.

1.1 Understand how visitors scan web pages

In the last few years, research has explored just how we read online. The Poynter Institute (a resource for journalists), the Estlow Center for Journalism and New Media, and Eyetools (a company which makes equipment for following eye movement) have been especially active in this field. In 2002, they joined to release the Eyetrack III study.

Eyetrack III observed over 40 people while they read online news sites. It found that they tended to start in the upper left-hand corner, moved from left to right, went to the bottom of the page, and then went back up the right-hand column.

Some of the Eyetrack findings were surprising. For example, larger type encouraged scanning; smaller type encouraged careful reading. Readers paid attention to blurbs if they were on the same line as the headline. Blurbs were read more often when they were short and the first two words grabbed attention. Readers paid attention to text first and photos second.

Other findings were predictable. Short paragraphs got twice the number of "eye fixations" as long paragraphs. And stories displayed in a single column (instead of two or three columns of text displayed across the screen) got more attentive reading.

Readers also liked summary descriptions introducing articles. These "decks" are longer than a regular blurb, but got 95 percent viewing even in boldface or italic typefaces — which are notoriously hard to read in long passages. What's more, people who read decks went on to read just as much of the article as when they read articles with no decks.

More recently, Jakob Nielsen conducted an eye-tracking study on many different kinds of websites, not just news sources. He found an "F-shaped" reading pattern: visitors would start at the top left, scan straight across, return to the left, drop down, and scan to the right again. Then they'd return to the left side of the page, going straight down.

Nielsen concluded that users don't read text very thoroughly. The first two paragraphs must give the most important information (very much like a news story). Subheads, paragraphs, and bullets should start with information-carrying words.

These findings tend to confirm an idea long known to business writers and tabloid journalists: we usually pay most attention to text at the beginning and end of a sentence, and especially to text at the beginning and end of a paragraph.

If these "hot spots" carry strong information, they deliver a stronger jolt to the reader. Writers of bad-news letters use this principle when they bury the bad news ("we can't hire you"; "we're not compensating you") in the middle of a paragraph, with neutral information at the beginning and end.

The implications are clear. Text containing long paragraphs has fewer hot spots, so on a website it delivers fewer jolts. Many visitors also recoil when they see a big block of text — finding it repulsive. Short paragraphs made of short sentences have more hot spots, and therefore more jolts. In general, hit-and-run readers will prefer the high-joltage sites.

1.2 Treat every page like a front page

A pop song of yesteryear might well be the anthem of webwriters: "Shut the door, they're coming through the window."

Web surfers can directly access just about any page on your site that doesn't require a password. You can create a detailed, well-organized front page with a clear statement of your site's purpose and a good table of contents. But if I ask a search engine to find pages that mention snowboarding, and one of your other pages features the word "snowboarding," I may go to that page without ever seeing the rest of your site, let alone your front page. I won't even know much about your site unless you give me information and navigation aids on your snowboarding page.

Every page on your site should at least have a link to your front page or display a table of contents. In that way, readers who have entered your site "through the window" will at least know where they are and what else your site has to offer. The terms you use in the table of contents should be identical to the headings you have used in the text. Your readers want to find their way around your site with the least possible confusion. If each page has consistent, clear navigation cues, readers will be grateful.

Many sites now offer both a table of contents and a site map that provides a direct link to each individual page on the site. A site map may not have room for blurbs, but it's a good idea to at least group pages into sections. So if your website on the town of Chesterton has a page for each hotel in Chesterton, list those pages on the site map under a section on Lodging, not in alphabetical order by hotel name interspersed with all the other site map entries.

1.3 Signal transitions with navigation buttons

In print text, paragraph indentations signal new topics or subtopics. Punctuation marks define relationships between words and phrases. And transitional words and phrases (e.g., meanwhile, secondly, nevertheless, a day later, another argument) let readers know how each sentence connects to the previous one. In hypertext, such transitions are generally meaningless because readers may jump from section to section in various sequences.

Linear text often prepares us for sequences:

Your journey through Mexico will include stays in Cuernavaca, Puebla, and Acapulco.

When we read sentences such as this one, we expect descriptions of each city, in the order given. Hypertext can prepare us for such sequences only by some cue outside the sequence, such as navigation buttons labeled <u>Cuernavaca</u>, <u>Puebla</u>, and <u>Acapulco</u>.

Your front page may include both links to different sections of your site and links to specific passages within a single page — especially if it's a long, scrolling page. You can also create such links at the top of a long page. This allows readers to skip up and down the page to the paragraphs they are most interested in.

Be careful about the directional terms you use to label your navigation buttons. Your readers aren't all arriving at your site via your front page. If Google brings your readers straight to your Puebla page, a navigation link that says <u>Back to Home Page</u> doesn't make much sense. How can they go "back" to some place they've never been? Why have a button that says <u>Next</u> if the page it links to has nothing to do with Puebla? It would be better to create navigation links that say <u>To Mexico Home Page</u> or <u>To Acapulco Page</u>.

If you are working with long, scrolling documents, provide ways to jump to the beginning and various sections of the document at the bottom of the page, and perhaps at intermediate stages:

<u>To Top of Financial Aid Page</u>

<u>To Chesterton College Policies Page</u>

<u>To Chesterton College Home Page</u>

Most websites today have a fairly standard layout: a banner giving the site's name, a string of links from left to right under the banner, and another string running down the left-hand side. Still, readers may find navigation a bit confusing until they become familiar with your particular layout. You may do them a favor with some guidelines in a prominent spot: <u>Read Me First</u>, <u>Introduction</u>, <u>If You're New to This Site</u>, or some such cue.

2. Orientation: Headlines

The term *headlines* can include the title of your site (the banner), the titles of individual pages, and subheadings that break up text. Like the thesis sentence of a paragraph, headlines tell us what to expect, so take some time to make them meaningful.

Ideally, the title of your site should tell readers what it's about: In Praise of Holly Cole, or Your Guide to Chesterton. Many of your readers will find you through a search engine that gives them the site title and the first few words of text. If your title is Paradise!, and your introductory text is "Here is the land the conquistadors sought," readers searching for Chesterton may not realize this is the site they've been looking for.

If you're skilled in HTML, you can write a meta tag that some search engines will display instead of the first few words on your page. A keyword meta tag lists words and phrases that searchers might use: *skiing, snowboarding, winter sports, hiking, alpine environment, recreation.* Some sites load such keywords (invisibly) onto their front pages so that search engines will display the sites in the first batch of "hits" the engines turn up. Many search engines, however, will reject sites with lists of meta tags: if they find the word *skiing* repeated ten times in an invisible meta tag, the engines recognize that this is an attempt to get the site to the top of the list of hits, and will not display the site.

If you don't know how to create meta tags, don't worry. Just make sure the keywords that readers are likely to search for are in your title and the first few lines of text. Search engines will usually include those lines in their lists of hits.

Keep your headlines close to the text they introduce. Usually, headlines, including subheads, should be just one double space from the first line of regular text that follows.

2.1 Use subheads

The Eyetrack III study found that subheads encouraged skimmers to stay with an online news story. That seems generally true for any kind of webtext. If you're writing and organizing your text in screen-size chunks, subheads will prepare readers for the content that is to appear in the following chunk.

Since readers tend to scan website text rather than read from line to line, each subhead is a kind of landmark. It tells readers what they will find in each section. Again, they save time by scanning for the subhead that they want.

You may even find that a single chunk of 100 words can still benefit from two or three subheads. A solid mass of 100 words, in eight or ten lines, does not invite reading. It needs at least a headline. The text should break into two or more paragraphs, with perhaps a subhead somewhere near the middle of the chunk.

The layout and formatting of subheads in webtext is much like that in print. Subheads tend to be boldface (or in color, or both), with white space above and text close below. In a two-line subhead, the second line should be shorter than the first. If you've broken your text into chunks or clickable pages, every subhead ought to have at least five or six lines of body text following it before the end of the chunk or page.

If you're providing long, scrolling text, subheads will help to break it up into manageable lengths. If the document is over 1,000 words long, break it up with subheads and create links to those subheads at the top of the page:

Financial Aid and Awards

General Information   Services of the Financial Aid Office

Scholastic Awards   Deadlines for Applications

Emergency Funding   Publications

Your readers now have the choice of scrolling through the whole text, or jumping to particular sections of interest.

2.2 Hook readers' interest: Hooks, links, and blurbs

For a word less than 100 years old, *blurb* has gone through some remarkable changes in meaning.

American humorist Gelett Burgess coined the term in 1907. He sketched a voluptuous blonde as cover art for a book jacket, and named her "Miss Blinda Blurb." For some time, sexy cover art was referred to as a "blurb," but the word also came to mean any overdone praise appearing on the book jacket.

While that is still an accepted meaning, pulp magazines of the 1920s and 1930s used *blurb* in a different sense, meaning the brief summary of a story appearing between the title and the text. (Print editors today more often use the word *deck* for this summary.) Its purpose was to tempt readers into investing the time to read the story.

On the Web, we now use blurb to mean a notice about what to expect on the other side of a link. Like the pulp magazines, we want our readers to make that jump and invest some time in our text. They are more likely to do so if they have a sense of what they're getting themselves into. Without any clue, they may be reluctant to wander into the labyrinth. In effect, we haven't given them adequate orientation to our site.

A link on a front page should have two parts — a hook and a blurb — though both may appear as a single word or phrase. The hook — a term borrowed from magazine writing — is introductory words that grab reader attention. In our case, the hook is usually the text of the link itself: <u>Best Snowboarding in Colorado</u>, or <u>Typical House Prices in Lynn Valley</u>. If you think these descriptions are enough to motivate readers to click on the link, then fine. Bear in mind that you have a wide range of hooking devices to choose from:

- **Quotation Marks.** "We love to read text that someone is supposed to have actually spoken," says Crawford Kilian.

- **Question.** A question promises an answer, and we'll jump through the link to find it.

- **Unusual statement.** Anything surprising will give your readers a jolt and make them wonder what other bizarre things you may have to say.

- **Comparisons/contrasts.** Comparisons show how things are similar; contrasts show how they differ.

- **News peg.** A tie-in with a big current event can draw interest (but don't let the news peg go stale on you).

- **Promise of conflict.** An attack or refutation makes us want to read more.

- **Direct address.** Web writing needs the "you" attitude, so talk directly to the reader.

- **Rebuttal.** Disagreement means a fight, and we all love to watch.

These hooks may stand on their own, but sometimes you're trapped with text that may be confusing or ambiguous. I teach in a Communications department, and I get a lot of mail intended for our public-relations people (who work in what's called "College Relations"). What if you're trying to show the difference between your company's Information Systems department and your Information Services department? That's where a blurb comes in handy:

Information Systems

Computer support, webmaster, staff training.

Information Services

Public relations, technical editing, company newsletter, advertising purchases.

Even if your text link seems self-explanatory, a blurb may make it more inviting. Maybe your text link is <u>What makes a good business plan?</u> The implied promise of an answer becomes more explicit with a blurb such as: "Six successful entrepreneurs offer practical advice."

Whatever hook you use, make sure it's appropriate. A blurb promising conflict, for example, had better deliver the conflict.

Subheads are especially helpful in selling. They can gain attention (Free!), spark interest (How to retire in two years!), and make readers act (Click here for your instant subscription).

You can also make life easier for your readers by turning both hook and blurb into additional links. Suppose you have a link to <u>Company Personnel Policies</u>. Make the jump and you find yourself on a page full of still more links. Give readers the chance to go directly to the policy they want:

Company Personnel Policies

Policies dealing with <u>Hiring</u>, <u>Probationary Period</u>, <u>Employee Evaluation Procedures</u>, <u>Health and Safety Issues</u>, <u>Conflict Resolution</u>, <u>Salary Scale</u>, etc.

If screen space permits, you can break the blurb into a bulleted list or columns; the point is to guide readers where they want to go, as quickly and conveniently as possible.

Fight the urge to turn the blurb into a mini-essay. The blurb should always be the shortest you can possibly make it. If the word, phrase, or sentence enables readers to use the link confidently, its job is done.

The blurb might also indicate whether the text on the other side is an archive (a text originally written for print on paper) or a chunk (a text of no more than 80 or 100 words designed for hit-and-run reading). Many news sites do this when they display a headline and the first paragraph of a story, with <u>(Full Story)</u> at the end. You might do this with your company's annual report, with a summary in chunk form and the blurbs <u>Full Text in PDF</u> and <u>Full Text in HTML</u> as links.

With a link to chunked text, the blurb can simply make the link more explicit (again guiding readers where they want to go):

Student Tuition Fees

Fees for the 2007-2008 academic year for <u>resident</u> and <u>international students</u>.

Whatever page your readers land on, they should have the opportunity to respond to what they find — and to you. An email link may seem self-evident, but it might get more traffic with a blurb:

<u>crof@shaw.ca</u>

I'd love to hear your opinion of this advice!

3. Information: Analyze Your Audience — and Yourself!

Are you looking for customers, converts, students, employers, kindred spirits? Are they experienced in using the Web, or complete novices? Do they speak English? Do they read it? To find out, you'll need to do some research and soul search.

In some cases, you can draw a detailed demographic analysis based on careful research. Maybe you're selling package tours to singles aged 18 to 34, or providing medical advice for parents of children with cystic fibrosis, or celebrating a pop singer who appeals to girls aged 13 to 17. Much of what you have to say — in both content and style — should reflect what you know about that readership.

In other cases, your subject will cross boundaries of age, gender, and nationality. Your audience will care about the research you've put into the subject, but it would be impossible to do similar research into the audience itself. This is where research yields to soul search: you need to ask yourself what other fans of Holly Cole would really like to find on your site, or what information would excite potential applicants to your college's computer-animation program.

Whatever decisions you make about the nature of your desired audience, don't forget that many in that target group simply don't have access to the Web, or don't even know about your site. Meanwhile, many other people who are not among your desired audience may turn up out of curiosity or by accident. Presumably you want them to leave with a good impression of you, your organization, and your typical audience, even if they're not especially interested in the content of your site. So even if your site is highly specialized, it should offer something to the casual visitor.

Meanwhile, think seriously about your own reasons for creating or revising the site. Are you aiming to make money, attract tourists, recruit supporters, or share an interest?

3.1 What's your exformation?

Let me explain "exformation" with an anecdote:

One day long ago, my grandfather and his friend Will Crawford (for whom I was named) went for a walk in the woods of rural New Jersey where they lived. On their return, my grandfather (who would later gain notoriety as the "Fernwood Flasher") exclaimed to my grandmother, "We must have seen a million rabbits in the woods!"

Uncle Bill, standing behind him, held up one hand, fingers outstretched, and silently mouthed the word: Five.

Ever since then, when someone in my family exaggerates, someone else will hold up a hand and repeat Uncle Bill's silent five.

We don't have to repeat the whole story because we all know it. Almost every family and every group has some short-hand communication — a running gag, a child's baby-talk name preserved as a nickname, a word used in a special way. People in the northern California village of Boonville even developed a local dialect, "Boontling," back in the 1920s. After one young couple was caught *in flagrante* on a pile of burlap bags, the Boontling word for making love was "burlappin."

Terms like these, once understood, become extremely effective. They seem to pack an extra emotional punch. The smaller the cue, the more powerful the response. Five upheld fingers are a devastating retort to some long-winded claim.

But to get the impact, you don't send a lot of information — you send almost none. Instead you rely on the knowledge you share with your reader or listener.

Danish writer Tor Norretranders, in his book *The User Illusion*, invented a term for this: *exformation*. Exformation is short for "explicitly discarded information," the information you strip out of a message because you know your reader already has it. The more you share with your reader, the less you have to say.

Norretranders's prime example is a communication between the French novelist Victor Hugo and his publisher. On holiday just after the publication of his novel *Les Misérables*, Hugo sent the following telegram to his publisher: "?"

To which his publisher replied: "!"

The anecdote would of course lack all meaning, never mind emotional impact, if I hadn't supplied the background (the information).

For webwriters, exformation is a big problem. How much of our text assumes shared knowledge? How much do we need to spell out? And is our exformation the same as our readers'?

Several years ago I gave a seminar on webwriting, using the second edition of this book as the text. Everyone in the group was Canadian, except one — a Brazilian woman who didn't understand the title of the first chapter, "Hype and Hypertext." What, she wanted to know, was "hype"?

Like a carefully explained joke, *hype* had lost most of its punch by the time I managed to translate the term. (And you'll notice I've changed the title of Chapter 1 in this edition.)

3.1a Exformation and unity for a global audience

The Web is a medium that thrives on jolts. Strip all but the absolute minimum information out of your text, and your readers get a major jolt if they share your exformation.

But what if your readers come from all over the world, and from different generations? How much knowledge you share with them is uncertain, but you know they're on your site looking for jolts, not long-winded explanations of one-liners. Explaining too much is almost as bad as explaining too little — it implies you think your visitors are ignorant.

Well, sometimes they *are* ignorant, and they do need to know the information that you've explicitly discarded. How to do it?

If your text is technical, or uses regional dialect, or has lots of unusual idioms, one solution is to create a glossary. Each unusual or difficult expression can be a link to its definition. Those sharing your exformation can skip the links; those who need the definition can make a quick hop to the glossary and then hop back again.

If your site is intended for those who read English as a foreign language, or who are trying to learn a technical vocabulary, you can simply include an explanation or definition in the text, or make it clear from the context. But what seems clear to you may be opaque to your readers, so it's wise to test your text before you put it before the world.

A third approach is one I've used in this section. Remember that I said my grandfather became notorious as the "Fernwood Flasher"? Some of you, if you recall the 1970s TV sitcom *Mary Hartman, Mary Hartman*, may remember that Mary's grandfather was a demented old man who went around in a raincoat, exposing himself. You would have instantly seen his

image in your memory, even if you didn't recall his name —
Victor Kilian.

Write in Global English

Only about one-third of Internet users are native English speakers — a much smaller proportion than in the 1990s. English is widely spoken as a second language, but nonnative speakers have trouble understanding some kinds of usage.

Rachel McAlpine, a New Zealand webwriting expert, has published a book titled *Global English for Global Business*, and you can find the basics of Global English on her website at www.webpagecontent.com/corp _archive/139/5/.

One of the great advantages of Global English is that it's good webwriting for everyone. Short sentences with few fancy words make life easier for all readers of webtext.

3.2 Create a "client brief"

In some cases, when you're creating the content for someone's site you need the most specific guidance you can get from your client. Even if you're writing text for your own personal site, your job will be easier if you have a clear idea of the image you want to convey. Here are some questions that a typical client brief might include:

1. **What are the short-term and long-term objectives of the site?** For example, do you want to promote immediate online sales to visitors who will become repeat customers?

2. **What are the demographics, values, attitudes, and lifestyles of your desired audience?** If you're aiming at under-30s but your cultural references and values statements are all straight out of the 1960s, you're in trouble. (Take the "Environics 3SC Survey" at http://3sc.environics.net/surveys/3sc/main/3sc.asp to get a sense of your own social values.)

3. **What personality traits should the site convey through its tone and manner?** A breezy style on a site for public-health professionals may drive away the visitors you want. But a personal blog should convey your own personality, whether breezy, angry, or meditative.

4. **What do your current visitors think of the site in its present form?** If you don't know, you'd better find out. A brief, easy-to-do survey could save you a lot of time and trouble.

5. **What is the general impression you want visitors to gain after they've spent some time on the site?** If you're a freelance accountant, you certainly want visitors to think you're highly skilled, very professional, and easily accessible.

6. **What kinds of content will foster a positive perception among visitors?** Maybe it's constant updates, or archives of hard-to-find historical data, or documents and forms that make it easy for visitors to do what they came for.

7. **About how much of your current site can be reused?** And do you need to revise or edit that old content? This question can force you to look at existing content much more critically, instead of shoveling it back in just because it's available.

8. **What are your desired start and completion dates?** These should be realistic but not too generous — a looming deadline can inspire more work than a far-off one.

9. **What activities would you like visitors to take part in on the site?** Do you want them to join chats, put items in a shopping cart, take a quiz, download materials?

10. **What "gifts" or services can you offer visitors?** Web culture loves free stuff, so even a business site should give away something — if only a ticket for a 10 percent discount on your first purchase. Special-interest sites often form "rings" that enable visitors to jump to related sites. Such visitors clearly appreciate the service.

3.3 Organize consciously

Don't throw material into your site at random, just because it's hypertext. You have several possible ways to organize your content.

3.3a Narrative order: What happens next?

Narrative order involves describing a process through time. If it's a fairly extended narrative ("My Six Months Backpacking Through Africa"), you might as well make it a single long document and treat it as a downloadable archive. If it's a short narrative, or breaks logically into subsections, it might work better in chunks.

For example, if you're describing the process of home brewing, each stage might get its own page. Readers can go to the page they're interested in without having to scroll through material they don't want. However, readers may want to print out the text explaining the whole process, so you could make it available as a single document elsewhere on your site. (Be sure to let readers know that it's available.)

3.3b Logical order: Appeal to reason

When you present text in logical order, you make an assertion, you bring in documentation to back it up, and you come to a conclusion. This may get long-winded, so your arguments are likely to end up at archive length rather than in short, powerful chunks.

If you're really familiar with the Web, you may be tempted to simply mention your sources and turn them into links:

A famous American scientist, <u>Linus Pauling</u>, started the modern craze for vitamin C as a cure-all.

If you do this, however, your readers may surf away to the Linus Pauling home page and may not return to your site. A more useful approach for citing sources is to put your links to sources at the end of your argument, the way scientific journals do. That way, readers will finish reading your argument and then visit your sources if they are interested.

3.3c Categorical order: Any way you want it

Hypertext comes into its own when text is organized in categorical order. You have a subject that breaks more or less obviously into chunks, with no particular reason to list chunks in a specific order.

To spare your readers from navigation problems and information overload, you have to impose some kind of order on your categorical material. Maybe your site has a page with links to five other pages describing the five most popular trails in your regional park. You could list them from shortest to longest (or vice versa), from north to south, from easiest to hardest, even in alphabetical order. The blurb on the front page could indicate how you've organized them, from shortest to longest, for example:

<u>Alpine Meadows Trail</u>. 6 km. Really steep, but what views!

<u>High Corniche Trail</u>. 18 km. For experienced hikers only.

Readers will then use your blurb as a guide to the trails that most interest them.

3.4 Writing webtext from scratch

If you're simply transferring a print document (such as a company report or a park brochure) to a website, imposing categorical order on your material will not be an issue.

But if you're generating your own text, you may feel baffled trying to sort it all out. You want to present coherent, easy-to-follow text, but your mind operates like simmering minestrone soup: ideas float to the surface, then sink again. Try to force organization on your own thoughts, and you get the cerebral equivalent of a system crash.

"Clustering" is one effective way to begin ordering your material. It's a simple process for outwitting yourself. First, let the ideas of possible topics to include on your website come into your head in whatever order they like, and jot them down as they occur to you.

One idea inspires another; write that down too. Eventually you have several sheets of paper (or a computer screen) covered with ideas in no particular sequence.

Now that those ideas are out of your head, you can look at them and see which belong together. Some are clearly introductory; others deal with the main subject; still others are part of the conclusion.

Cluster these ideas by tagging all the introductory items with a #1 or an A. The central ideas could be tagged #2, #3, #4, or B, C, D; the concluding ideas, #5 or E. If you're doing this exercise on a word processor, you can drag the ideas into the appropriate clusters, and before you know it, you're organized.

Suppose you're putting together the website for Chesterton, a year-round sports and sightseeing destination. You might start jotting down ideas something like this:

> history, skiing, snowboarding, zinc mine, logging, motels, hotels, youth hostels, regional parks, shopping, wildlife, environmental problems, swimming, waterskiing, hiking trails, entertainment, restaurants

Obviously, some ideas inspired related ones, but most topics just occurred to you more or less at random. You see some obvious categories: Winter Sports, Summer Sports, Lodging. In the Winter Sports category, you could put skiing and snowboarding — and, come to think of it, you can also put in something about snowshoeing and ice skating.

Later on, you may want a separate page for Winter Sports, or you may decide to lump them in with other activities in a Year-Round Sports section.

Clustering works for almost any kind of writing task, and in webwriting it also suggests how you might design your navigation system. Maybe each section of your text will have its own navigation button on your front page. Or, if you're creating a long, scrolling page, a contents list at the top of the page could provide links to each section.

When you are organizing your information and text, keep your readers in mind. If you know your site will get mostly hit-and-run readers, your pages should display concise chunks of text. If you're planning a "library" of long documents for readers looking for detailed information, then you won't have to edit yourself quite as harshly.

You will also want to consider how you want readers to respond to a particular item: with a click to some other chunk, or with an email answer? And will they get a suitable reward for their trouble? Webwriting, like chess, means you have to think several moves ahead — and put yourself in your readers' shoes.

3.5 Style and display

You should be generating your webtext in whatever font and size are comfortable for you. You know that your readers may have set their monitors to display some other default font, in some other size, and you can't control that. You also know that PCs and Macs may display your site somewhat differently. But you can ensure that your readers at least come close to seeing your text as you wish them to.

First, bear in mind that a serif font, like the one used in the main text of this book, is usually easier to read in extended text than a sans serif font, like the one used for headings throughout this book. However, some sans serif fonts like Verdana and Trebuchet were designed for the computer screen, and they work well also.

So if you have long passages of text, a serif font (or a screen-designed font) is your best bet. Point size makes a difference too. Usually, type should appear no smaller than 10 points and no larger than 14 points. Readers with poor eyesight will especially prefer larger point sizes.

Stick with plain text. Use capital letters, small caps, italics, and boldface sparingly. The purpose of these special displays is to emphasize something; the more displays you use, the less emphasis anything will get. A whole paragraph in *italics* or SMALL CAPS or REGULAR CAPS will be hard to read.

Combining special displays only makes matters worse. A headline in **BOLD *ITALIC CAPS*** is overkill. If you must use all uppercase letters, scale down the point size a little. And don't even think about underlining for emphasis; on the Web, an underline means a link.

Remember that a font such as 12-point Georgia is great for reading on a monitor but may be awkward as a printer font. For example, a table may not print correctly because 12-point Georgia makes the table too big to fit on a letter-sized page.

A web author can specify a particular font and size right in the HTML code of the site. As long as the font is one that readers have on their computers, the site will appear more or less as the author wants it to. But if the font isn't on the reader's computer, or the reader has chosen to override a website's font, the reader's default font will take over — perhaps with disastrous results for display and readability. You should probably leave decisions about display up to your readers.

Be very careful about mixing colors. If you choose a black background and then display text in dark blue, you are going to make your site unreadable. The same is true of light colors, such as yellow text on a pale-green background. Good old black text on a white page should serve you well for most purposes. Your web authoring program will usually let you specify the colors you want for your text and background. In general, your text should be as dark as possible and the background color (if any) should be pale.

Unless you intend your archived material to be printed out rather than read off the screen, try to avoid running text the full width of the monitor. A column about half the width of the screen is much easier to read because no line will be much more than ten words long. Any longer, and readers will have trouble finding the beginning of the next line.

3.6 Format for Printing

Your readers may want to use your text both onscreen and on paper. Anyone who has tried printing from the screen, however, finds that not all documents look the same on paper. If you intend or expect your text to be used in both media, you can make readers' lives easier by avoiding certain practices:

- A wide multicolumned table can pack a lot of information into a single screen, but the reader's printer may not pick up the whole table (especially if the browser is set to display a big screen font and the reader hasn't remembered to switch to a printer font).

- Hyphenated words can make your screen text look tidy, but the hyphens may carry over into reformatted print text, where they become needless errors. Better to use a ragged-right margin with no hyphenation at all.

- Page number references usually become meaningless once a web page is printed, as do navigation cues such as <u>Next</u> and <u>Back</u>.

3.7 Use Bulleted Lists

As readers, we're used to sentences on paper with long lists of nouns, verbs, and phrases. On the monitor such sentences become harder to read — and harder to respond to. This can be a problem in an interactive medium such as the Web.

Bulleted lists, used properly, can help convey information quickly and keep your readers on the page. Instead of plodding through long paragraphs, they can grasp the key points at once.

Bullets, then, have several functions for webwriters:

- They focus attention on important points.

- They organize the content, often serving as a preview or summary of material.

- They improve the design of your page.

Compare the following almost unreadable paragraph with the bulleted form that follows it:

The media have given us some of their own occupational slang, like "sound bite," but trendy clichés usually come from the occupations and professions most studied by the chattering classes. So business has given us bottom lines, deep pockets, and downsizing. The military has given us bite the bullet, in the trenches, breakthrough, and flak. Engineering gives us parameters, state of the art, leading edge, and reinventing the wheel. Athletics gives us team players, ballpark figures, level playing fields, and track records. Politics is the home of charisma, spin doctors, bandwagons, and momentum. The self-help movement gives us trendy clichés like self-actualizing, holistic, meaningful, one day at a time, and wellness.

Revised for the Web:

The media have given us some of their own occupational slang, like "sound bite," but trendy clichés usually come from the occupations and professions most studied by the chattering classes:

- *Business:* bottom lines, deep pockets, downsizing

- *Military:* bite the bullet, in the trenches, breakthrough, flak

- *Engineering:* parameters, state of the art, leading edge, reinventing the wheel

- *Athletics:* team players, ballpark figures, level playing fields, track records

- *Politics:* charisma, spin doctors, bandwagons, momentum

- *Self-help movement:* self-actualizing, holistic, meaningful, one day at a time, wellness

Bulleted lists offer a couple of other advantages: You don't have to keep finding different ways to say the same thing (Business has given us, the military has given us, athletics gives us), and it's easier to sound objective.

Keep bulleted lists parallel in form. That is, make every item a sentence ending in a period, or make every item a similar kind of phrase, without end punctuation.

Bulleted lists should be short. Six or seven bullets (as in the example above) are probably the maximum. One bulleted list per chunk or screen is enough.

Bulleted lists may introduce a longer discussion of the topics mentioned, or may provide links to other sites dealing with the topics.

Think about the length of the items in a bulleted list. If each item is actually a full paragraph, you're losing the impact of bulleting. Use subheads instead. And if each item is just a single word or a short phrase, the list should also have just three or four items.

And a small point: You have a huge number of bullet types to choose from — black circles, boxes, check marks, and so on. Keep your bullets simple and discreet. Exercise 1, at the end of this chapter, will help you practice converting prose into bullets. (All the exercises in this book are also included on the CD-ROM.)

For an excellent guide to using bulleted lists, see Kim Long's *Writing in Bullets: The New Rules for Maximum Business Communication* (Running Press, 2003).

---

4. Action: Communication Runs Both Ways

In Chapter 1, I talked about standard and interactive communication models. Many people still think the one-way, standard model is the only one, and they use postal and ballistic metaphors to describe what they do as communicators.

These metaphors are unfortunately still common in business and education. Teachers still "deliver" courses like so much junk mail, while politicians and businesses "target" voters and consumers with messages that "get through" like armor-piercing bullets. And to reverse the metaphor, governments launch cruise missiles at other governments to "send a message." The basic premise is that communication is a monologue, valuable only to the extent that it creates the desired effect.

If you design your website as a missile-launching platform aimed at passive readers, you're missing the whole point of the Web. No matter what you put on your site, it's worthless until readers arrive, construe your meaning, and act on your information (assuming you've made it possible for them to act).

Your readers, not you, will decide what your site really means and what value it has. You in turn have to respond to what your readers tell you, and before you know it, you're engaged in a conversation. If you listen to them and respond by adapting your content, you too are being interactive.

If you don't listen and don't adapt, your site is just a waste of time and bandwidth.

4.1 Response cues

Since the Web is supposed to be an interactive medium, your readers should respond to the information you provide with more than "So what?" You want them to take action.

Often, the only action needed for readers is to follow a link to another page, so the only response cue you need to provide is a clear link title and perhaps a blurb. But you may also want a more specific response: an email message, the submission of a form, a purchase order.

As marketers in the print media know, many people are slow and reluctant to respond on paper: they have to find a pen, and then an envelope, and then a stamp, and then they have to go out in the rain and mail their response. This is why so many companies provide stamped envelopes and some kind of bribe or threat — all simply to prod customers to respond.

Response is far easier on a website. Click on an email address and an email form pops up; just type in a few words, click on the Send button, and you're done. A form would be even easier — just reply to questions by clicking on the buttons. Worried about transmitting your credit card number over the Web? Just provide your telephone number, and the organization you want to order from will call you.

Easy as response may be, most users still don't respond — especially if it means spending money. We'll look at marketing in more detail in Chapter 8, but for now, let's just put ourselves in the readers' shoes. What's in it for them if they email you, fill out your form, join your listserv, or answer your questionnaire? Presumably they get some sort of reward, a benefit or pleasure they would otherwise miss out on. And they have to know they'll miss it!

So invite your readers to act in their own interest:

Just fill out this form to make sure you get regular updates on Holly Cole's concert tour — plus a chance to win a copy of her latest CD!

To reserve your beautiful room at Chesterton Lodge — at 10 percent off season rates — just send us your telephone number and we'll call right back to get your credit card number and confirm your reservation.

If you want current news about the market for romances, you'll be glad you joined HEARTMART-L, the listserv for professional and aspiring romance novelists. All you need to do is send us an email. Market news and tips will start arriving within hours!

This survey has 40 questions and takes only 10 to 12 minutes to complete. You'll be automatically entered into our contest for a free weekend at the Chesterton Lodge.

You can make a difference! Let your government representatives know what you think by adding your name to our email protest. They'll know in minutes that you're angry and you want results!

Notice that each invitation tries to make action sound effortless: "Just fill out this form," "All you need to do," "They'll know in minutes." The action needed is built right into the appeal through a link to the suitable form. The Web is a culture of impatience, so effective appeals offer quick and painless ways to respond.

5. Reviewing a Website

We usually understand a problem better (and find solutions faster) when we can discuss it in detail. If you look at your webtext in progress and all you can say is "This sucks!", you're not likely to improve it until you can identify the problem.

Reviewing someone else's site can help. The purpose of a website review is to enable you to identify the key elements of a site (both concept and execution) and, thereby, to identify what may help or hurt your own site.

You may want to develop your own review criteria, which could include some or all of the following:

- **Purpose.** Is the website for entertainment, marketing, information, or education? Is the purpose achieved? How? If not, why not — has the author misjudged the audience or misunderstood the nature and conventions of the Web?

- **Audience.** Is the site for novices or for the experienced? Are they young or old? Male or female?

- **Content.** Is the site information-rich or just a jump page? Hit-and-run or archival? Does the content live up to the site title or blurbs? Is the text clear, well written, and well organized?

- **Appearance.** Does the site have good graphic sense? Do graphics enhance content or just decorate?

- **Accessibility.** Does the page load quickly?

- **Organization.** Is the site easily navigable? Does it require lots of scrolling? Lots of page jumps? Do you find "link rot" (links that go nowhere)? Is there any confusion about where Back or Next might lead?

If you can articulate your responses to good and bad websites, you'll be able to do the same for your own — and others who review your site will have more kind things to say about it.

Exercise 1
Converting Prose to Bullets

Convert the following paragraph to a bulleted list. Compare your version with the one in Appendix 5 at the back of the book.

Science fiction evolved from earlier genres and has kept some of their conventions. These include an isolated society, whether an island, a lost valley, or a distant planet; a morally significant language, such as Orwell's Newspeak; documents that play an important role in the story, like the Book of Bokonon in Vonnegut's *Cat's Cradle*; an ideological attitude toward sex, as in Huxley's *Brave New World*; and an inquisitive outsider, like Genly Ai in Le Guin's *The Left Hand of Darkness*.

[80 words]

_____

_____

_____

_____

_____

_____

_____

_____

_____

_____

4

WRITING GOOD WEBTEXT

You have two main sources of material for your site: brand-new, self-created text, or text from other sources (e.g., annual reports, résumés, and technical memorandums). When you're importing text from print sources, you may have little choice: the site may simply be the archive of items that have to remain exactly as written. But in some cases, you may indeed have to adapt text from other sources to make it easily usable on your site.

Unless you've done very little writing for print, you're going to bring all kinds of habits from the print medium. That's fine; much of what goes on your site will end up on paper anyway, and the basics of good writing are the same in any medium.

Let's consider those basics in the light of the two information principles mentioned in Chapter 2:

- **Clarity:** Webwriting should be understandable at first glance.

- **Correctness:** Webwriting should reflect proper English usage and appropriate nonverbal messages.

To make sure that your writing is understandable at first glance, and that your writing is correct, consider the following suggestions.

1. Activate the Passive

The passive voice is an occupational hazard in many fields: science, technical specialties, academic writing, and bureaucracy are all rich sources of the passive voice. It's so common that most writers in such fields don't even know when they're using it — and if they do know, they're actually proud of themselves for doing so. They think they sound professional.

In the active voice, you always know who's doing what:

I studied the novels of Ursula K. Le Guin.

Pol Pot massacred hundreds of thousands of Cambodians.

Tim Berners-Lee invented the World Wide Web in 1989.

Most readers are very comfortable with the active voice, but in technical and bureaucratic writing, the active voice can draw unnecessary attention to the writer or actor:

I tested 33 subjects for Ebola fever.

The inspectors found several minor infractions.

You made a serious mistake.

Technical and bureaucratic writers tend to avoid this kind of attention. They prefer to write:

Thirty-three subjects were tested for Ebola fever.

Several minor infractions were found.

A serious mistake was made.

This puts attention on the action, not the actors, and sometimes that's exactly what you want. It also appears more objective, because the actors disappear, or turn up at the end of the sentence in a prepositional phrase:

Several minor infractions were found by the inspectors.

A serious mistake was made by the captain.

For writers who want to seem objective, and therefore more credible, the passive voice is dangerously attractive. That's because people who use passive voice a lot are likely to use it where it doesn't belong. Imagine your partner saying about your cooking: "Dinner was greatly enjoyed by me." Imagine yourself replying: "Your comments are very much appreciated." You'd both sound like stuffed shirts, and if you write your webtext in this way, your readers will think you really are a stuffed shirt — or at best a dull and wordy writer.

Sometimes, of course, you really do want to keep attention on the act, and not the actor. Maybe it's more important to mention that a mistake was made, without blaming anyone in particular. In those cases you should use passive voice — but use it consciously, when it serves your purpose, not just because you think it sounds professional.

Don't confuse passive voice with past tense. If you write "I enjoyed dinner," you're using active voice and past tense. If you write "Dinner was enjoyed by me," you're still in past tense (dinner happened in the past), but you're also in passive voice. The person who did the enjoying is lost in a prepositional phrase ("by me") at the end of the sentence, instead of being the subject at the beginning of the sentence.

Passive voice raises another problem for webwriters: it means more words. "I enjoyed dinner" is three words; "Dinner was enjoyed by me" is five. You are asking your reader to plow through two extra words for no good reason.

Use Exercise 2 at the end of this chapter to practice using active voice.

2. Choose Concrete Anglo-Saxon Words

If you are conversant in English, you have the incredible luck to speak and write a language that falls in love with every other language it meets. English will borrow words from other languages all over the world, and then forget to return them.

English speakers weren't always so promiscuous (to use a Latin word). When Roman missionaries first converted Britons to Christianity, they had to translate *crux* (cross) as *rood* because their converts preferred their own Germanic language. But when the French-speaking Normans conquered Britain, they imposed their Latin-based language on the country. So the French *croix*, from Latin *crux*, became the Modern English "cross." French and Latin were the languages of culture and law. Words from Anglo-Saxon Old English tended to stay in the mud of the barnyard.

We now have two main streams in English: words from Latin (and Greek), which we use for technical, scientific, bureaucratic, and scholarly writing, and Anglo-Saxon words, which we use in everyday conversation.

Greco-Latin words tend to be abstract and hard to visualize. Anglo-Saxon words are concrete and easy to visualize. When we "cause collateral damage," it's hard to understand that we are "killing unlucky bystanders." In some cases, the Latin word has largely replaced the Anglo-Saxon one and we're stuck with the Latin. If we talk about "folks in North Carolina" instead of "people in North Carolina," we're going to sound a little too casual: "people" comes from Latin and "folks" is Anglo-Saxon.

On balance, though, Anglo-Saxon words are more immediate and understandable than Greco-Latin ones. Unless you're writing for highly specialized readers on a topic with a Greco-Latin technical vocabulary, choose the Anglo-Saxon word over the Greco-Latin one. (Most good dictionaries will list the origin of a word — OE means Old English, for example, and Gk means Greek. The definition may also give a more usable synonym for a rare word.)

Use Exercise 3 at the end of this chapter to practice using Anglo-Saxon Words.

3. Use Simple Sentences

Depending on their organization, sentences can be simple, compound, complex, or compound-complex. Here are examples of each:

- **Simple sentence:** This website celebrates the career of Holly Cole (subject: "website," verb: "celebrates").

- **Compound sentence:** This website celebrates the career of Holly Cole, and it also provides links to other Canadian singers' sites ("and" links to second subject, "it," and second verb, "provides").

- **Complex sentence:** This website celebrates the career of Holly Cole, who is a Canadian jazz singer (simple sentence with a subordinate clause attached — "who is a Canadian jazz singer").

A subordinate clause is one that can't stand on its own; it must be part of an independent clause, which is a complete sentence.

- **Compound-complex sentence:** This website celebrates the career of Holly Cole, who is a Canadian jazz singer, and it also provides links to other Canadian singers' sites (two independent clauses, linked by "and," with one independent clause modified by a subordinate clause).

You'll probably agree that the first sentence, the simple sentence, is the easiest to read. The longer a sentence becomes, the harder it is to read. Short, simple sentences will be much easier for everyone to understand quickly.

This is especially important for text on your front page, where many readers will first arrive. If that page is a solid mass of complex text, stretching clear across the screen, many readers will simply surf on to somewhere else. If your front page is just a brief introduction to the site's topics, plus a table of contents, simple sentences (and even phrases) are all you need.

Don't feel you have to write in a dumbed-down style, though. By all means vary your sentence patterns, if only to hold reader interest. But most sentences should be short and simple, with an average length of 20 words or so.

What if you're archiving long texts written in a complex style? Fine — your readers will probably want to download them to read later, either onscreen or as printouts.

4. Avoid Clichés

Avoid clichés like the plague. A cliché is a phrase or expression that was once so new and surprising that everyone repeated it. Like an unspoiled tourist destination ruined by too many tourists, the cliché loses its whole reason for existence when everyone uses it.

Clichés have several forms. Proverbial clichés include "a stitch in time saves nine," "too many cooks spoil the broth," and "an ounce of prevention saves a pound of cure." Sometimes you can get away with using such clichés by letting readers know that you *know* you're offering a stale but barely usable term: "Here's the proverbial ounce of prevention that will save you a pound of cure." This sentence may still be hard for people to understand if they've grown up with the metric system.

Slangy clichés have the embarrassing look of someone who thinks the 1970s are still happening. When you read terms such as *uptight*, *outasight*, and *far out*, you're dealing with someone in a time warp (if that's not a cliché too).

If you're very careful you may be able to get away with dead slang if you use it ironically. *Kewl* for "cool" is an attempt to do so — though not a very successful attempt. (Scholars of slang may recall that before *cool* took over in the late 1950s, the "hepcats" described anything they really admired as "real George." That one, at least, died a merciful death.)

Trendy clichés are a little different. Slang tends to come from marginal groups like ethnic minorities; trendy clichés come from the mass media's journalists and commentators, the "chattering classes" (there's a trendy cliché in itself). People who write or speak for a living tend — to use yet another cliché — "to drink each other's bathwater." One of them will come up with an unusual word or phrase, and everyone else seizes on it. Before you know it, everyone on CNN or the editorial page of your local newspaper is talking about *interfaces*, *closure*, and *empowerment*.

When you look at a website, pay attention to the text. Does it resort to clichés or jargon? Of what kind? What is the effect created by the clichés or jargon? Can you imagine why the writer used them? And can you imagine how the text might read with the clichés removed?

You might try downloading text from a site and then revising it to remove all clichés. You're likely to find that your version is much stronger and more effective than the original.

5. Choose Strong Verbs over Weak Ones

A hazard of business writing is the tendency to take a good, strong verb and turn it into a noun or phrase — and then to put a weak verb in its place. Consider the following:

Make a decision	Decide
Conduct a survey of	Survey
Make allowance for	Allow for
Make use of	Use
Do a review	Review
Perform a test	Test

The first phrases are longer, and may sound better to some people, but choose the shorter ones unless you have an urgent reason to write the longer version. At least think about why the longer term would be better before you use it.

6. Be Aware of Dialect Variations

A dialect is a form of a language specific to a particular region that most local residents can generally understand, but which they may not use themselves. So a Scot from Edinburgh and an Australian from Melbourne will be able to converse in English, but they won't speak in the same accent or with quite the same vocabulary.

In different English dialects, the same word can mean different things. In American English, a *bluff* is a low cliff; in Canadian English, it means a grove of trees on the prairie. And different words can mean the same thing. In Standard English, for example, *flaunt* means to show off, and *flout* means to break a rule in public. Most North Americans, however, will talk about someone "flaunting the law," but they don't mean waving the constitution around — they mean publicly breaking the law. In their dialects, that's what flaunt means. This may be incorrect Standard English, but it's perfectly understandable even to Standard English speakers.

The problem is that non-Standard usage may distract readers from the message. (In fairness, speakers and writers of Standard English may seem stuffy or pedantic to others. However, Standard remains the most widely understandable and accepted dialect.)

If you intend your website strictly for people who speak your own dialect, or you're trying for a strong local flavor, you can ignore Standard English. If you're trying to reach a broad audience, however, Standard English is your best choice. If you're unsure about what's considered Standard, countless manuals on English usage are available. Look in your library's reference section or a large local bookstore. Many dictionaries also include sections on grammar, spelling, and punctuation.

When in doubt, choose Plain Language

For a quick and useful introduction to Plain Language, visit www.plainlanguage.gov — dedicated to making the US federal government understandable.

---

7. Be Precise

You may also mislead your readers by choosing a word that's not quite what you mean. Suppose you're writing text for the Chesterton website and you decide to put in a link to current weather reports and forecasts. Do you call it Chesterton Climate Report or Chesterton Weather Report?

Well, *climate* refers to weather conditions over a period of months or years; *weather* refers to what's going on at the moment. Chesterton may have a dry climate, but it may also be expecting a downpour tonight. Be sure to choose your words precisely.

8. Don't Use Extended Metaphors

In print text we may develop an argument through contrast and comparison — that is, by showing how two things are different or similar. Again we use transition words and phrases:

> *Unlike the dungeons,* the castle's main floor is well furnished.

> *Just as in Cuernavaca,* your hosts in Taxco will make you feel very welcome.

In hypertext, as Robert E. Horn advises in his book *Mapping Hypertext*, we can use such contrasts and comparisons only within a single section. The same is true of extended metaphors. In a print document, you might describe a government as a "ship of state," with the executive as the bridge, the legislature as the engine room, and so on. This extended metaphor may work to help unify a passage of many paragraphs. But in hypertext, with readers skipping around in no predictable order, their first encounter with such a metaphor may be baffling.

9. Use Clear Antecedents

Hypertext must always include the antecedent for every pronoun in a given chunk. If I write, "She went on to earn a PhD in physics at MIT," I'd better mention her name earlier in the same chunk; otherwise readers won't know who "she" is.

In some cases, especially in fiction or articles using fiction techniques, the pronoun may come first — but the proper noun should follow close behind. For example:

She opened the door and switched on the light. Everything in her office seemed just as she'd left it. But Jane had an uncomfortable sense that someone had been here.

10. Grammar and Usage: Common Errors

Whether you're in New Zealand or New York, chances are you make the same errors in Standard English. This section discusses some of the most common errors.

10.1 Sentence fragments

Your sentence will be a fragment if it lacks a subject or a verb. Here are some examples of fragments and their corrected versions:

Which surprised everyone.	This surprised everyone.
Really weird.	I think that's really weird.
A superb musician but a troubled human being.	She was a superb musician but a troubled human being.
Not bloody likely!	That's not bloody likely!

Sentence fragments are often fine in captions and blurbs, where the reader doesn't really need a full sentence. So a tag such as "Joe Doakes in happier days" under a photo of Joe is all your readers require. A button linking to photos of your wedding can read <u>The Big Day!</u> instead of <u>Come This Way to See Photos of Our Wedding Day</u>.

However, in text where you're trying to explain or describe something in detail, avoid sentence fragments.

10.2 Subject-verb agreement errors

It's easy to make your verb disagree with your subject if you forget which word is your subject. For example:

> The leader of the frightened soldiers were unable to make them cease firing.

Because "soldiers" is close to the verb, many people might make the verb plural ("were") to agree with it. But look again — it was the soldiers' leader, not the soldiers themselves, who couldn't make them stop firing. The correct verb should be singular ("was").

In other cases, we have a compound subject but we mistakenly treat the two nouns like a single unit:

> Snow and sleet makes hiking dangerous on these trails. (The verb should be "make.")

> Spelling and grammar is my big problem in English. (The verb should be "are.")

In both of the above examples, the verbs should be plural to agree with the compound subjects. In some cases, however, we really can treat a plural as a singular:

> Six months is the standard probationary period.

> A million dollars is still a lot of money.

> Richards and Johnson is a distinguished law firm.

In these three examples, the subject is singular even though it could, in another context, be plural. In the first case, we use "six months" as a single unit of time. We can regard "a million dollars" as a unit of money. "Richards and Johnson" is a proper name that we can regard as a singular name for a company — just as we could say "The United Auto Workers is a large union."

And just to make things really confusing, sometimes we can describe a single thing or person with more than one noun and we still use a singular verb:

The lawyer and human-rights activist has enjoyed great success. (one person with two titles)

The singer and songwriter has won a Grammy. (one person with two skills)

If you're worried about subject-verb errors and you're not sure which noun is the subject, ask yourself: Who or what is performing the action of the verb in this sentence? Who's enjoyed success? Who's won two Grammys? The answer is your subject.

10.3 Incorrect pronouns

We use pronouns to stand in for nouns when repeating the nouns would sound awkward:

Dora released her latest video last month, and she says she's happy with it.

Imagine using Dora four times in that sentence:

Dora released Dora's latest video last month, and Dora says Dora's happy with it.

We sometimes run into trouble when we forget that some pronouns are subjective (that is, they are the subjects of the verb in the sentence) and others are objective (they receive the action of the verb).

He emailed her. She emailed him.

We'd laugh if we read:

Her emailed he. Him likes she a lot.

But many people, in conversation and in writing, will say:

She emailed him and I.

Me and her went to the conference.

Her and her husband set up a home-based business.

Evidently they think that the rules don't apply if they're talking about more than one person! But the rules do apply:

She emailed him and me.

She and I went to the conference.

She and her husband set up a home-based business.

Another pronoun problem is *myself*, which some people use incorrectly. Pronouns with "self" are either reflexive or emphatic:

I asked myself a question. (action of verb turns back on the asker)

I myself told you it wouldn't work. (emphasizes who told you)

Don't use *myself* as a long-winded way to say I or me:

Joan and myself went to the conference.

My wife and myself set up a home-based business.

10.4 Misuse of adjective for adverb

Adjectives modify nouns: a *good* man, a *fast* computer. Adverbs modify verbs, adjectives, and other adverbs: a *truly* good man, a *really* fast computer. Sometimes you can change the meaning of a sentence by using (or misusing) some common adjectives: "You did good by winning the contest" is incorrect, but "You did good by raising flood-relief money" is correct. We do well when we perform with style and excellence. We do good when we make the world a better place.

These are just four common grammar and usage problem areas. For details on these and many other hazards of usage, spelling, and punctuation, consult almost any composition handbook or dictionary.

Exercise 2
Activating the Passive

Revise these sentences to activate the passive voice and then check your answers against those in Appendix 5 at the back of the book.

1. It is argued by some researchers that alien bodies were retrieved by the US Air Force from a crashed spacecraft near Roswell, New Mexico, in 1947.

   _____

   _____

   _____

2. Miles Davis's *Sketches of Spain* was hailed by critics as one of his finest works.

   _____

   _____

   _____

3. Graphical user interface was originally developed by researchers at Xerox.

   _____

   _____

   _____

4. A cholera outbreak in 19th-century London was stopped when a neighborhood water pump's handle was removed by a local physician.

   _____

   _____

   _____

5. These graphics have been chosen carefully to illustrate each step of the process.

   _____

   _____

   _____

Exercise 3
Using Anglo-Saxon Vocabulary

Replace each of the following words with an Anglo-Saxon word or phrase (or a more common Greco-Latin word):

1.	altercation	_____
2.	antagonist	_____
3.	capitulate	_____
4.	celestial	_____
5.	demotic	_____
6.	epitome	_____
7.	fiduciary	_____
8.	gravamen	_____
9.	impediment	_____
10.	litigious	_____

Compare your answers with those in Appendix 5. If you can't find a shorter, clearer word without checking your dictionary, imagine how your readers would feel if they didn't have a dictionary at all. Now that you know these words, do your readers a favor: Don't use them in your webtext!

5
EDITING WEBTEXT

I n ancient Rome, the title of the person who sponsored a gladiatorial fight to the death was *Editor.* Maybe because of that association with hacking and slashing, modern writers are often suspicious of editors. They shouldn't be. A good editor can save you from countless embarrassing mistakes while helping you make your points more coherently, more eloquently, and even more gracefully.

What's more, you can be your own editor. Here are some steps you can take to improve your own text once you've drafted it.

1. Don't Trust Your Spell Checker

Computer spell checkers are rubber crutches: they fail just when you need them most. All they do is compare what you've written with a list of words, and if they find the word in their list, they say it's okay. So you may have written "their" when you meant to write "there," or "your" when you meant "you're," and the spell checker will tell you it's correct.

The spell checker will of course catch outright typos, doubled words, and other errors, so it has some usefulness. But a quick skim of your document, flagging obvious goofs, is the best you can hope for from a spell checker.

If you have a grammar and style checker, you're a little better off, but not much. Style checkers can spot bad habits such as overuse of the passive voice or too many prepositional phrases. This at least forces you to think about whether you want to indulge in such habits.

2. Check Your Reading Level

Your style checker can also give you a sense of the reading level of your text. It does so by counting the number of syllables per word, the number of words per sentence, and the number of sentences per 100 words. The reading level, usually expressed as a grade level, goes up as words, sentences, and paragraphs get longer. (This book is readable at the Kincaid grade 7 level, for example.)

If your site is aimed at a general audience, especially one including young children or persons who don't read English fluently, it's common sense to keep the reading level as low as the subject permits. You don't get extra points for making your text readable only to PhD candidates. And as Albert Einstein once said, "If you can't explain it clearly, you don't understand it well enough."

I got a powerful lesson about readability a few years ago when I typed a chapter from the book of Ecclesiastes into a

Word file and then checked its readability. Even with its verses compounded into two- and three-sentence paragraphs, Ecclesiastes came out readable at the grade 3 level.

How readable are you?

For a really detailed analysis of your text, go to Readability.info (www.readability.info). You can either upload a Word file or enter the URL of your website. You'll get seven different readability scores, with an explanation of them.

Readability.info also gives you the number of sentences and their length, and the number of paragraphs plus number of sentences in the average paragraph. This can help you identify unconscious writing habits.

---

3. Cut Verbiage

Your hit-and-run text is all that most of your readers will bother with. Only really dedicated people will actually look at your archived text and perhaps download it for careful reading. Therefore your hit-and-run text should be as brief as possible, so it delivers its message clearly and quickly.

If you set yourself an arbitrary word limit — for example, no chunk of text may run over 75 words — you will be amazed at how easy it is to cut the fat out of your text.

As a first step, deliberately write long chunks of text: maybe 150 or 200 words. Then start cutting words until you're down to 55 or 60 words. Now you have the luxury of actually adding some words. Every sentence, every phrase, every word has had to fight for its life. Nothing is there just because it sounds good — you're writing, remember, not making music! You've packed the maximum meaning into the minimum text, so your readers will get the message in the shortest possible time.

Use Exercise 4 at the end of this chapter so you can practice cutting verbiage and adjusting a text's reading level.

4. Critique Your Own Text

A writer lives inside your head, and so does an editor. They don't always get along. Your inner writer is having a great time being creative and showing off his vocabulary; your inner editor is watching over the writer's shoulder and tearing her hair out. While the writer is cranking out Great Prose, the editor is screaming herself hoarse about what drivel this all is.

The writer doesn't hear the details, but starts feeling nervous. "Maybe this isn't all that good after all," he mutters. Finally he decides something's gone horribly wrong (heaven knows what), and he abandons the job.

Sound familiar?

It doesn't have to be that way. If you were a best-selling author, you could send your messed-up manuscript to your high-priced editor, who would tell you exactly what was going right and wrong with the manuscript and offer detailed advice on improvements. What if you don't have the services of a professional editor? Well, you have an editor living right inside your skull — all you have to do is give her a chance to put her criticisms into words.

So as you're putting your webtext together, keep a diary or journal in which you can make notes to yourself about how your writing is going. If a problem does arise, your inner editor can sound off about it ("The introduction is way too long and too cute, and we don't need to use the word *fiduciary*").

Once you've put the problem into words, something startling happens: a solution follows almost instantly. When you start organizing your ideas into sentences and paragraphs, the process seems to free the creative part of your mind, and it comes up with answers that you'd never get if you just pounded your head against the edge of your desk. Sometimes the answer comes before you've finished writing the sentence describing the problem.

Self-critiques don't just help with problems of style. Your inner editor may also warn you about problems in the organization of your site. Maybe you want to list numerous excellent links to other sites on your front page; your editor, if you give her the chance, will tell you not to do that. Instead, "put them down in the basement so readers don't find them until they've looked at all our own stuff."

5. Print Out to Proofread

You simply cannot trust your own proofreading abilities unless you proofread from paper. Not only is computer-screen text hard to read, it's hard to proofread as well. That means it will be very hard for you to catch your typos if you're proofreading only on the screen. The longer you try, the less accurate you'll be because monitor reading will tire you out. Your readers, however, will come to your site fresh and unfamiliar with your text. So they'll spot those typos every time. Your text may look subliterate even if it's only mistyped.

Sections that you haven't changed much as you've added to your website are especially dangerous. On my first website, I didn't look at my headline after I'd written it; when I installed the site, the headline featured an embarrassing typo — which I didn't catch until *after* I'd invited dozens of colleagues to take a look.

When you print out your site text to proofread it, don't print it out in 10-point single-spaced text. Make it 14-point and double-spaced, use an unfamiliar font, and let it sit overnight before you proofread. That way your text will look unfamiliar. You'll have to read what's actually on the paper, not what's on the inside of your forehead — and errors are more likely to leap out at you.

Here's another useful tip: read your text out loud. That will also force you to read every word, instead of just skimming. You may find some awkward phrases that looked okay on the screen and on paper, but that sound clumsy or suggest an unintended meaning. Better to catch them now and correct them before showing your site to a global audience.

Does this sound like a lot of hassle for a humble little web page about your favorite singer or your dog-walking service? Maybe so, but typos, bad grammar, and other mechanical errors can really hurt the impact of your page. Maybe you can create amazing sounds and graphics, but if you can't spell, your readers will notice — and they won't like it.

This is especially true when you have a business site promoting either your own skills or the virtues of the company that's hired you to write content for its site. Simple proofreading mistakes instantly make you look bush league and unprofessional.

6. Don't Respect the Text

Maybe we have an ingrained respect for the written word that originated in ancient Babylon when only the sacred priests were literate. Maybe it just goes back to the days of the manual typewriter, when a minor error or afterthought meant re-typing the whole page. Whatever the reason, we revere text too much. It gives us a dangerous readiness to dump print-for-paper onto a website and think we've done our job.

Respect for text is bad enough for print-media writers; on the Web, it's disastrous. In print, we expect readers to skip right along from point to point. If our text is wordy or complex, we rely on readers to get the point pretty quickly anyway. Maybe we even tell ourselves that our ideas are so subtle and nuanced that only an elaborate style will convey them adequately.

On the Web, readers need only hit the Back button to dismiss our illusions. If we want to attract them, hold them, and inspire them to react to what we've said, we need to look at our text with a cold, dispassionate eye.

Jakob Nielsen told us in the 1990s that low-resolution computer monitors slowed down reading speed by up to 25 percent. Screen resolution is improving, but many computer users still rely on old computers and small laptops. As mentioned earlier, in his new book *Prioritizing Web Usability*, Nielsen predicts most of us will have large, high-resolution monitors by 2009.

But until then, everything we adapt from print to screen should be at least 25 percent shorter. Print-media text assumes readers will sit still for a long, interwoven argument; when surfers find such arguments, too often they just surf on to somewhere else. And when that happens we've squandered the great advantage the Web gives us as writers: the chance to engage our readers in dialogue.

Some print materials, of course, don't need adaptation because they're simply archived on the site. An annual report, a survey, an article once published in a newspaper — these can remain at full length. As PDF (portable document format) files, they can even retain their original formatting.

But for visitors who are simply scanning your site, you should try to provide a smorgasbord, with everything available at a glance. To make scanning easier, you need to adapt most print texts by including the following:

- Self-explanatory titles on your contents pages, so scanners will know what they're heading for when they click through.

- Blurbs, in case the titles really aren't all that self-explanatory.

- Headings that either form titles for individual chunks of text, or divide even a single screenful of text into two or three segments.

- Condensed text that conveys the key elements as concisely as possible — perhaps with links to the original-length archived item for those who want every detail.

The condensation process demands utmost disrespect for print-source text. A useful guideline is to cut such text by not just 25 percent, but 50 percent, just to see if it's possible. If the result can't stand on its own, then restore some of the original text (or a concise version of it) until a visitor, arriving directly on this chunk, will understand what it's about.

And not only understand it, but respond to it! Maybe you want your readers to respond by jumping to the archived original, or emailing your organization, or buying the product. Whatever the response desired, the text should make it an easy, attractive choice. What's more, the choice itself should spark a positive response from the website:

Congratulations! Your first email newsletter is on its way! Let us know what you think of it.

Thank you for your purchase. It should reach you within 48 hours. Meanwhile, your user manual is already in your mailbox.

Maybe you feel awkward about disrespecting the text, but what's really important is that you give utmost respect to the visitors who have honored you with their presence on your site. Whatever you can do to make their visit interesting, surprising, and successful — including presenting text as clearly and concisely as possible — should make it clear that their needs come first.

7. Edit for International Readers

When you write for the Web, remember that it really is worldwide. Many readers may be native English speakers, but most Web users are not. Even native speakers may have trouble with particular dialects. For example, a "car smash" in Memphis is a "fender bender" in California. When an Australian man has a "mate," it's his male friend and not his wife.

If we're going to meet the needs of our worldwide readers, we must make our language as simple and clear as possible. This isn't easy. Recently I asked a Chinese pen pal for her snail-mail address; she sent me her Hotmail address instead — because she thought *snail mail* must mean an email account that opens very slowly.

Does this mean that we have to set our grammar checkers to flag anything that might make a third-grader frown? Do we have to define every word?

No — at least, not usually. For example, the other day I referred a foreign student to my college's website for advice about admissions and fees. The information for foreign students isn't written very simply. The rationale is that if its readers can't understand routine college-level English, they're not yet ready for admission to college.

Similarly, foreign professionals may be very much at ease with the technical English of their profession, even if their colloquial

English is awkward. So a technical site need not oversimplify its content.

In some cases, you may even want to emphasize your dialect. A Canadian site can offer an exotic *flavour* to American visitors if its writers *labour* to spell British-style. It can also use distinctly Canadian terms, like *saltchuck* for salt water and *bluff* for grove of trees. If your site's dialect is likely to baffle too many visitors, however, a glossary may help.

Many readers will grasp unfamiliar terms just from context, but the context can be blunt or subtle:

> We went out on the saltchuck, which is what some British Columbians call salt water.

> We went out on the saltchuck, braving choppy waves in our sea kayaks.

So for technical sites, or "exotic sites," specialized dialects will be fine. A site designed for general readers, however, should probably use Standard English — a vocabulary of widely understood words with very few regional, slangy, or idiomatic expressions.

Am I being a terrible spoilsport who disapproves of having fun with English? I should hope not! As George Orwell said in the last of his rules for clear English: "Break any of these rules sooner than say anything outright barbarous."

And don't forget one priceless advantage you have as a webwriter — you can encourage and provoke your readers to ask questions about the unusual words and phrases on your site. Your content isn't just a take-it-or-leave-it box lunch, but a constantly changing buffet of interesting and sometimes mysterious items. If customers find you eager to explain what's on offer, they'll be delighted to learn and experiment — and you'll learn how much you still have to learn about your own language.

8. A Webwriter's Style Guide

In print media, style guides don't interest rank amateurs or literary geniuses. Amateurs don't know the rules; geniuses break them.

But for professional writers, style guides are as necessary as tape measures and plumb bobs are for carpenters. This is especially true if you're responsible for designing and maintaining a corporate or advocacy site where both appearance and language should be correct and consistent. When several persons are writing for one site, it's helpful to have a guide to "house style."

Several style guides already exist for the Web, though they're more honored in the breach than the observance. Sir Tim Berners-Lee, the father of the Web, created such a style guide. So did Gareth Rees (though I believe his guide is now available only as an appendix in this book).

If your site caters to specialists with their own dialect or technical shop talk, your style guide can be descriptive, reflecting your readers' usage — even if it's not really "correct" English.

But many style guides should prescribe everything from abbreviations to precise word usages. Newspapers and publishers use such guides for the sake of consistency, and to save their writers and editors from repeatedly researching every obscure question. I can recommend several for North American webwriters:

USA:

The Chicago Manual of Style, 15th edition. University of Chicago Press, 2003. Website: www.chicagomanualofstyle.org

The Associated Press Stylebook and Libel Manual, ed. Norm Goldstein. Perseus Press, 1998.

The Microsoft Manual of Style for Technical Publications, 3rd edition. Microsoft Press, 2003.

Canada:

The Canadian Press Stylebook: A Guide for Writing and Editing, 14th edition, ed. Patti Tasko. Canadian Press, 2006.

The Canadian Style: A Guide to Writing and Editing. Dundurn Press, 1997.

Editing Canadian English, 2nd edition. Macfarlane Walter & Ross, 2000.

Guide to style guides

For basics about developing your own personal and consistent website style guide, visit Edit-Work (www.edit-work.com). It's not an active site, but the material there can be very helpful.

See Jeffrey Zeldman's style guide for A List Apart (www.alistapart.com/contribute/styleguide/) for an example of how to specify everything from the use of metaphor to the use of commas.

For an example of a style guide for a newspaper's blog, see "Telegraph blogging style guide" at http://blogs.telegraph.co.uk/upload/may06/styleguide.htm. The BBC News Styleguide (www.bbctraining.com/pdfs/newsstyleguide.pdf) should be helpful also.

The Economist offers a style guide at www.economist.com/research/styleguide/.

Do guides simply impose print standards where they don't belong? Such guides set limits to expression in a medium that — in theory — requires no such limits at all. Some might even argue that style guides force newcomers to adopt the vocabulary and tone of the Web's privileged early adopters.

I doubt it. Mavericks are still free to ignore (or attack) "correct" style in their preferred Web genres. But for the vast majority of users, consistent style within Web genres is as critical as consistent navigation.

What follows is a brief guide mixing both descriptive and prescriptive guidelines. I've emphasized Web-related expressions and terms that may be useful for both native English speakers and those for whom English is a foreign language. Some usages are standard whether in print or in webtext, and ignoring such usage will only distract or confuse your readers. Web jargon and slang can be especially baffling to newcomers, whether English is their native language or not. In other cases, expressions that seem vivid and fresh to you may be baffling or boring to others. In such cases, you should at least think carefully before using them.

8.1 Abbreviations

We use short forms of many words and phrases. Some are true abbreviations, while others are acronyms or initialisms. CA and Calif. are both abbreviations of California. UNESCO (United Nations Educational, Scientific, and Cultural Organization) is an acronym; we pronounce it as a word.

Sometimes acronyms become acceptable as words themselves, like scuba (self-containing underwater breathing apparatus) and radar (radio detection and ranging). FBI (Federal Bureau of Investigation) and RCMP (Royal Canadian Mounted Police) are initialisms; we sound out each letter.

Some abbreviations may be so common that they need no explanation: UN, NATO, TNT. Even then, if you expect numerous international readers unfamiliar with English abbreviations, an explanation somewhere in your text may be helpful. If you feel you must use an abbreviation that your readers may not recognize, write out the whole term first before beginning to use the abbreviation:

He joined the National Research Council (NRC) in 1986.

In some cases, the abbreviation may need more than just spelling out. TNT stands for trinitrotoluene; better to say "TNT, a powerful explosive." When using abbreviations from other languages, an explanation is often useful:

Pemex, Mexico's national oil corporation.

Acronyms formed only from the initial letters should be all capitals: North Atlantic Treaty Organization = NATO. (However, some British practice allows Nato.) Acronyms formed from initials and other letters in a proper name take capitals and lowercase letters: National Biscuit Company = Nabisco. Acronyms formed from phrases don't take capitals: microwave amplification by stimulated emission of radiation = maser; radio detection and ranging = radar.

Unless a Greek or Latin abbreviation is universally used, use the English equivalent. Your reader will understand "that is" and "for example" much faster than "i.e." and "e.g."

In many cases, when abbreviations appear in text intended for a website, your readers will thank you if you translate them into plain English.

8.2 Punctuating abbreviations

Frequently used abbreviations tend to lose their periods — B.A. becomes BA, and U.S.A. becomes USA — but it's still correct to include them. Abbreviations with mixed capital and lowercase letters usually keep their periods, but mixed abbreviations that begin and end with capitals lose their periods. Geographical abbreviations used in postal addresses should not include periods because postal scanners have trouble with them. So snail mail addressed to British Columbia or California should display BC or CA with no punctuation.

An honorific or title before a name is usually abbreviated (in North America, with a period; in Britain, without) when the person's whole name is included: Prof. Zhu Minhua, Maj. Gen. Robert Smith, Mr. David Porter, Ms. Joan Acosta. (But *Ms.* often appears as *Ms* even in North America.)

A title does not appear before a name if a title follows the name:

Louise Fairfax, MD

John Hutchinson, PhD

When a sentence ends with an abbreviation including periods, only one period is needed. When a sentence ends with a question mark or exclamation mark, it follows the last period of the abbreviation:

Welcome to B.C.

Welcome to B.C.!

8.3 Pluralizing abbreviations

Simply add *s* to most abbreviations: MVPs (most valuable players), MIAs (soldiers missing in action), NGOs (nongovernmental organizations).

8.4 Abbreviating dates

International and governmental organizations tend to display dates as year/month/day: 2006/03/21 is March 21, 2006. Most people, however, prefer day/month/year (21 March 2006) or month/day/year (March 21, 2006). Abbreviated dates may be ambiguous: does 03/04/05 mean April 5, 2003, March 4, 2005, or April 3, 2005?

To ensure understanding, write out dates in full or use abbreviations for the names of months: Apr 3 2005, 5 Apr 2003.

Abbreviations of calendar eras usually appear as:

AD: Anno Domini

BC: Before Christ

BP: Before the present (generally taken to be AD 2000, so 6400 BP = 4400 BC)

BCE: before the common era

CE: common era

These last two terms recognize that not everyone using the Christian calendar is necessarily a Christian.

8.5 Biased terms

As a webwriter you may want to challenge your readers, but challenges shouldn't include gratuitous pokes in the eye. Terms that seem perfectly acceptable to you may be deeply offensive to others. Is that because you're okay and your readers are thin-skinned idiots? Or because you don't have enough respect for your readers to address them in a civil manner?

Excessive concern with political correctness can lead to euphemism and denial of reality. But I suggest that when you can use a term that won't offend your readers, you should choose it. Maybe you prefer *black* to *African-American*. But if people prefer to be called African-American, then that is the term you should use.

More specifically, consider the following guidelines for avoiding biased terms.

8.5a Avoid pointless or irrelevant personal information

The head of your company may be the mother of two, the skip of a curling team, a fan of F. Scott Fitzgerald, and a superb cook; none of that is relevant when she announces a stock split.

Similarly, identifying a charged criminal as belonging to a particular ethnic group does little to enlighten your readers and may tend to make them infer unfounded generalizations.

8.5b Avoid faint praise

"Women are better than men at routine, repetitious jobs" not only insults men but suggests that women aren't very good at varied and creative work.

8.5c Avoid gender bias

In recent years, *gender* has come to mean the cultural or social roles assigned to men and women, while *sex* means the physiological or biological aspects of males and females. Many occupational terms have a male or female suffix because of ancient tradition, not modern reality. Changing *chairman* to *chairperson* isn't always adequate, in part because it sounds so self-conscious.

Consider the following alternatives:

actress:	actor (though only some actors are eligible for a best actress award)
alderman:	councillor (unless the term is official)
any man:	anyone, anybody
aviatrix:	flyer, pilot

anchorman/ anchorwoman:	anchor
businessman/ businesswoman:	businessperson, manager, entrepreneur, merchant
chairman/ chairwoman:	chair, convenor, president
cleaning woman:	cleaner
common man:	average person
countryman:	compatriot
fireman:	firefighter
fisherman:	fisher (that may sound odd at first, but no one says "loggerman" or "carpenterman")
man a counter:	staff a counter, run a counter
man in the street:	ordinary people
mankind:	humanity, humans, people
man-made:	synthetic, artificial
manpower:	workforce, labor force, staff, personnel
policeman/ policewoman:	police officer, constable, deputy (unless the officer's sex is relevant, as when a woman suspect is improperly searched by a policeman)
salesman/ saleswoman:	sales representative, sales clerk, salesperson
stewardess:	flight attendant
waitress:	server, waiter
workman:	worker, employee

Gender bias can also turn up in singular pronouns:

Anyone who bikes without a helmet will eventually get his head examined.

The "generic" singular pronoun is supposed to be *he*, but in practice we often prefer *they* — as in "get their head examined." This of course sounds a little odd; how can you have a plural pronoun and a singular noun?

While it doesn't work all the time, pluralizing the antecedent can solve many such problems:

People who bike without helmets will eventually get their heads examined.

8.5d Be careful about sexual orientation

Gay and *straight* were originally homosexual slang terms that have become standard usage. It's pointless to regret the loss of gay as a synonym for "happy," just as it's pointless to wish that *fond* still meant "foolish." While gay can apply to both men and women, you'll be clearer if you refer to "gay men and women" or to "gays and lesbians."

Be careful with terms that may be semantically loaded: *heterosexism* and *homophobia* are terms that criticize antigay attitudes, and you should use them only when you can back them up. Otherwise they're just name-calling, like "fag" and "dyke." Gays may feel free to use such terms about themselves, but outsiders should not — just as your mother can use a pet name for you that no one else dare use.

Transgendered may mean either someone who lives as a member of the opposite sex, or someone who has actually changed sex. The latter may also be referred to as a *transsexual*.

Don't confuse *sexual orientation* and *sexual preference*. Sexual orientation has to do with whether one prefers people of one's own sex or not. Sexual preference has to do with preferring blonds or particular styles of making love.

8.5e Be careful with ethnic terms

Be very careful when using terms such as *ethnic*, *race*, and *visible minority*. Yorkshire pudding is ethnic food just as *kreplachs* and *papadams* are. If you intend to mean a group that's culturally, linguistically, or physically different from the majority, you may still be on dangerous ground. Don't forget your readers may be reading your words in Karachi or Kyoto, where you might be the very visible minority.

When you must refer to people by ethnic and racial terms, use the terms they prefer: not "Eskimo," but *Inuit* (singular *Inuk*); not "Negro," but *African-American* or *black person*. Should you capitalize words like *black* in this context? Some people do, but *White* looks odd. Stick to using such terms as adjectives, not nouns, and you can usually stay in the lowercase: "a native attorney," "a black poet."

Terms such as *African*, *Asian*, or *Oriental* are so broad that they become meaningless. Berbers and Bantus are both Africans; Tamils and Japanese are both Asians; in the age of the Pacific Rim, the Orient is really to the west of most North Americans.

If a term like *native* seems odd to someone whose ancestors have lived in a country for ten generations, consider *aboriginal* or *indigenous*. One Canadian term for "Native Indians" is "First Nations." Where possible, be as specific as possible: Not "A Montana Indian," but "A Montana Blackfoot."

8.5f Be careful with disabilities

Rather than referring to *a disabled person* (which sounds as if the person isn't even conscious!), use the expression "a person with a disability."

When you refer to persons with physical or intellectual disabilities, avoid loaded terms like *victim*, *afflicted with*, or *suffering from*. A child may "use a wheelchair"; the child should not be "confined to the wheelchair." Be careful also to distinguish between disability and impairment (generally caused by accident or genetics) and disease.

In the case of intellectual disability and disease, use terms as accurately as possible. Pop psychology has made psychiatrists of us all, but don't use terms such as *schizophrenic* or *bipolar* unless you really know what you're talking about. Again, put the term in a prepositional phrase: "a person with schizophrenia," or "people diagnosed with bipolar disorder."

8.5g *Be careful about age*

North Americans are sensitive about their age, which may explain why we like euphemisms: *golden ager* rather than *old person*, for example. Only an old person should feel free to use terms like "geezer" or "old fart," and even then it may be more distracting than amusing.

Young people feel patronized by the terms *kid* and *youngster*. Up to about age 16, they're "boys and girls." After that they're "men and women," or "young persons." If a person's age is important to what you're writing about, mention it:

John Chang, 19, is already a dot-com millionaire.

At 79, Alma Jones is running in her 20th marathon.

If age is irrelevant, don't mention it.

8.6 Capitalization

Consult a dictionary or one of the style guides mentioned for details on capitalization. What follows deals with some special cases that webwriters should be aware of.

8.6a Capitalize trade names

Someone left a Styrofoam cup and a box of Kleenex on the Xerox copier.

If Valium doesn't work, try a Zoloft. If that doesn't work, take an aspirin; in Canada, you should take an Aspirin.

NOTE: Companies holding trade names often prosecute writers who fail to capitalize them. This is to prevent the trade names from becoming generic and therefore available for any-one to use. This happened with brand names like Nylon, Lano-lin, and Cellophane.

Similarly, follow the manufacturer's usage in capitalizing high-tech brand names, even when these include capitals within the word (also known derisively as "StudlyCaps").

WordPerfect

PowerPoint

8.6b SI/Metric units

In Système international d'unités (SI)/metric terms, almost all of the abbreviations are lowecased.

10 km (kilometers)

50 g (grams)

10 ha (hectares)

25 mg (milligrams)

EXCEPTION: SI terms based on proper names take a cap-ital, and so do the abbreviations for Celsius and liter.

60 V (volts) — from Volta

100 G (gauss) — from Gauss

10°C (Celsius)

2 L (liters)

8.6c Capitalizing lists

If a bulleted list is grammatically part of the sentence that introduces it, listed items do not take capitals.

Chesterton offers you —

- great skiing

- superb snowboarding

- exciting mountain biking

- exhilarating whitewater rafting

- awesome rock climbing

If the list is made up of complete sentences, each listed item does take a capital.

Why visit Chesterton?

- It's got great skiing from November to April.

- It's got superb snowboarding.

- Mountain biking challenges everyone from novices to professionals.

- Whitewater rafting is the best in the country.

- Rock climbing is awesome, but not for the faint-hearted.

8.6d Compound words

When a new term, made up of two or more words, comes into the language, we usually write it as separate words — for example, *electronic mail*, or *Web site*. But we soon hyphenate it or shorten it, or both. Electronic mail soon became *e-mail*, and has already become *email* for many of its users. Web site is still common, but many people prefer *website*. *Web-site* is very rare.

While practice does vary on the Web, the following compound-word usages appear to be preferred by most current users:

email

web page

website

webwriter

In many cases, hyphens help to make our meaning clear, and we'd better use them. Consider, for example:

I resent your message.

I re-sent your message.

In the same manner, do we want "more advanced research" (additional programs like present advanced research), or "more-advanced research" (programs that go beyond what we're doing now)? Was she wearing "a light brown coat" or "a light-brown coat"? Is he "an old computer expert" (aged but technically up to date), or "an old-computer expert" (capable of fixing a Lisa)?

Many compound terms, when they serve as adjectives, take hyphens:

a 50-year-old rock climber

our day-to-day routine

she joined a well-established firm

When we turn such phrases around, we drop the hyphens:

the rock climber is 50 years old

we follow the same routine from day to day

her firm is well established

EXCEPTION: When a compound phrase contains an -ly adverb, don't use a hyphen:

an insanely great computer

a truly astounding event

the triumphantly grinning winner

And don't hyphenate a compound containing a comparative or superlative:

She is the least known but most influential editor in the city.

Flash is one of the more dramatic tools for Web creation.

8.6e Measurements and numerical terms

Americans are the predominant users of the Web, and Americans also use the medieval "imperial" measurement system abandoned by every other civilized nation. The Système international d'unités (SI) is the generally accepted version of the metric system. As a webwriter you should be able to supply measurement terms that are meaningful to both Americans and the other six billion people on the planet.

If your website needs to present measurements, and if you expect readers from all over the world, you should display terms in both SI and imperial units.

8.6f Numbers in general

In most cases, use words for numbers one through ten, and numerals for numbers above ten:

seven days, 14 links, one and only, 11 players to a side

If a number begins a sentence, always spell it out:

Fifteen men sat on a dead man's chest.

Six dollars will get you a ticket.

But if a number is part of an address, a title, a brand, or an organization's name, follow its usage even at the beginning of a sentence:

195 Kinloch Lane was at the end of the street.

7Up is a popular soft drink.

4587 Corporation is a little-known holding company.

When providing two different sets of numbers, use words for one and numerals for the other:

We have 6 two-bedroom suites, 1 studio apartment, and 4 three-bedroom suites.

Use a hyphen when writing out numbers between 21 and 99:

Thirty-nine students crammed the classrom.

One hundred and sixty-two emails arrived overnight.

Don't use commas with long, spelled-out numbers or mixed numbers:

Pay to the order of John Smith: One thousand two hundred fifty-five dollars.

He stands six feet 11 inches tall.

He covered the course in one hour 15 minutes 16 seconds.

9. Online Advice About Online Writing Style

Here are some websites that offer good advice about writing for the Web. Such sites usually offer still more links to additional resources. You can also find more resources by using search engines and keying in phrases such as "Web style" or "webwriting" or "writing for the Web."

- Tim Berners-Lee's CERN Style Guide: www.w3.org/ Provider/Style/Overview.html

- Jakob Nielsen, Writing for the Web: www.useit.com/papers/webwriting/

- Yale Center for Advanced Instructional Media, Web Style Guide, 2nd Edition: www.webstyleguide.com

- Joe Gillespie's Web Page Design for Designers: www.wpdfd.com

- Jeffrey Zeldman's A List Apart: www.alistapart.com

- Web Pages that Suck: http://webpagesthatsuck.com

- CIO Magazine: Content Management: www.cio.com/summaries/web/content/

Exercise 4
Editing Text for Websites

Here are some short texts that should be even shorter on a website. Edit them to approximately half their original length. You can remove individual words and phrases, or sentences, or even whole paragraphs. In some cases, a single new sentence can replace a couple of paragraphs.

Do your first edit on these pages. Then go to the original texts on the CD-ROM that came with this book and revise them to reflect your changes. Go to www.Readability.info and upload each revised text (as a Microsoft Word file). Your word count should be half of the original, and your readability level ("Fog Index") should be at least one grade lower.

1. **It's Your Choice**
    [Word count: 500, Fog Index: 9.3]

    It's your first day on the job, and here's your first task. Your boss hands you a check, made out to you, for $735,800.

    "Tear it up," says your boss.

    That's what you're doing if you never go to school beyond grade 12. According to Statistics Canada, the average 2001 income was $25,671 for British Columbians with grade 12 only, or with just a couple of post-secondary courses. Over a 40-year working life, that means you'd make just over $1 million.

    But if you go into the workforce with a university degree, your lifetime income will average $735,800 more. Your work is more likely to be interesting and secure, and you'll have more choices about when and how you do your job.

    So if you skip post-secondary, you're not just losing all that money — you're working in boring, insecure jobs, where someone else is always giving you orders. You're losing control over your own life.

In effect, the more education you have, the more choices you have. So how do you maximize your choices as you leave high school?

Start by going from grade 12 into academic post-secondary courses, whether at university or at your local community college. That gives you three choices: go on to more university, switch to a career program after a year or two, or go into the workforce, with the option of returning to school later.

Suppose you decide after a year or two of academic courses that you want some practical job training. Many college career programs now require a year or two of academic coursework before they'll even consider you. So you have more programs to choose from, and a better chance to be accepted.

If you take your academic courses in college, you can transfer to university — and you'll have saved money by taking that first year or two at lower tuition fees.

But what if you settle for a college diploma in some career field? StatsCan says your average income will be about $33,000, or $1.3 million over your working life. That's less than you'd get with a BA, but still pretty good (especially if you love the job). And many career programs now offer degrees as well, in fields like business administration and tourism management. So you still have plenty of choices.

You even have the choice of working while studying part time for a certificate or degree — and once you've got your degree, you may head back to college for a career-program certificate and some job-specific skills that will equip you for a wider range of careers.

Sometimes we don't have all the choices we'd like: We're not rich enough, we're not interested in academic study, we're living in the wrong place, we've got family commitments. Even so, if you think seriously about what you want to do with your life, you'll realize you do have at least some options. Which one to take? The one that reduces your future choices, or the one that increases them?

It's your choice.

2. **Those Who Can, Do. Those Who Can Do Really Well, Teach!**
[Word count: 520, Fog Index: 7.7]

If you're graduating this June, you're probably not thinking much beyond this summer: a job, some travel, a lot of partying, and then either more work or going back to the classroom in some college or university.

If you're going on to post-secondary next September, expect to be shocked: Your teachers are likely to be older than your parents. When you were born in the late 1980s, today's professors were already middle aged. If you go into a vocational or trades program, the same is likely to be true. And that means you have a fantastic opportunity ahead of you.

Forty years ago, the schools were caught in a tidal wave called the baby boom. A huge mass of kids (your parents) was moving through the system, and the schools were desperate to find teachers for them. A whole generation, born in the late 1930s and early 1940s, found that schools were always hiring. Teaching was "what you can always fall back on," they used to say.

The teachers hired in the 1960s and 70s are retiring now. We don't have a baby boom, but we do have an economy that needs lots of educated workers. So as old teachers retire, the system will need new ones — not just science and English and history teachers, but people who can teach the skilled trades as well.

A recent BC survey predicts that in the next few years we'll need 40,000 new workers in the natural and applied sciences. Ninety thousand jobs will be waiting for people in trades, transportation, and equipment operation. Sales and service will need 180,000 new workers.

Other high-growth job fields include everything from graphic design to nursing to management in accommodation, food, and retail. So your timing couldn't be better. When you come out of college or university, the jobs will be there.

But think about your choices. With so many jobs, you might as well pick a field you really enjoy — something that demands just the skills you get a kick out of using. People skills? Train for sales or management. Visual skills? Learn graphic design and multimedia. Love your car? Learn an automotive trade. No matter what you choose, some employer will be out there waiting to pay you to have fun.

That's not all. With employers fighting to hire the next generation of skilled workers, demand will be high for still more workers. Colleges, universities, and vocational schools will be fighting too — to find qualified people to teach everything from law to Chinese cooking.

If you really love your job, and you love showing people how to do it, you could have even more fun as a teacher. As a newly qualified skilled worker, you'll be familiar with current practices and technology. You can teach part time, staying in touch with the workplace. Teacher-training programs will be delighted to have you. You'll be training people who may be working alongside you soon, so you can make sure they learn what they should.

So pay attention to those old, old teachers in your courses next year. You may be stepping into their jobs before you know it.

3. **Adapting Print Text to the Web**
   [Word count: 300, Fog Index: 9.0]

Too many people use the Web like a billboard, pasting up documents designed as print on paper. While a website can certainly serve as an archive for such work, most Web surfers aren't looking for long print documents, and don't bother to read them.

They prefer to scan a screen of text, looking for keywords and interesting links, and they don't like to scroll. So a "chunk" of text, enough to fill a screen, is the basic unit of webwriting. It wouldn't be more than 100 words long, and may be much shorter.

To turn print text into chunks, it's a good idea to try to cut by 50 percent. So if your original text was 500 words, you should try to get it down to 250. Then you should see if you can break it into two or three chunks, each able to stand on its own. What's more, each chunk should be two or three short paragraphs. That's because a solid mass of text is hard to read on screen — especially when people prefer to scan rather than read line by line.

Webwriters have three jobs: They have to orient their readers so they can navigate around each page, and around the whole site. They have to supply information that's easy to find and understand.

And they have to enable readers to act on that information — to buy the product, subscribe to the email newsletter, join the club.

That's a tall order, all right. But if webwriters can't fill that order, their readers will soon be confused, or frustrated — and then they'll be gone to some other site. But simple navigation, useful information, and easy action will make any site worth visiting and revisiting.

4. Developing Efficient Work Habits
[Word count: 900, Fog Index: 10.3]

Different writers face different advantages and drawbacks in forming good writing habits. The circumstances of your personal life may make it easy or hard to find writing time, but time itself is not the real issue — it's habit. Writing must be something you do regularly, like brushing your teeth. The writer who waits for inspiration will wait even longer for a complete, published book. Writing habits flourish best in routine, but the efficient writer also exploits opportunity.

Routine: Set aside some time every day when you can work undisturbed for an hour or two — first thing in the morning, during lunch, after dinner, whenever you can set aside other demands. Ideally, it's the same time of day. Your family and friends will soon build their routines around yours. With luck, they will resent your unscheduled appearances during your writing time, and will send you packing back to your desk.

Keep your writing equipment (paper, pens, software manuals, etc.) in your writing place, close at hand. Minimize distractions such as interesting new magazines and books. Try to find a writing time when few people phone or visit. If a cup of coffee and some background music make you feel less lonely, by all means enjoy them.

Use household chores as thinking time: a chance to review what you've done so far and to consider where your writing should go next. Walking the dog or vacuuming the carpet can provide more ideas than you expect. This is really just "controlled daydreaming," letting your mind freewheel in a particular direction: what the opening should be in the next chapter, how to present both sides of a controversy. But the process doesn't seem to work if you just sit and stare at the wall. You need to be up and moving in some automatic pattern.

Don't lean on others for editorial advice and encouragement — least of all people you're emotionally involved with. Spouses, friends, and roommates rarely have both editorial perceptiveness and the tact to express it without infuriating you or breaking your heart. Empty praise will get you nowhere; unconstructive criticism can destroy your book in an instant.

Instead, *be your own editor*: set aside regular times to write yourself letters discussing your own work, articulating what's good and less good in it. In the process you'll easily solve problems that could otherwise grow into full-blown writer's block. On a computer, the letters can form a continuous journal, recording your reactions to the evolving work. Checking back to the first journal entries can help keep you on track — or dramatically show how far you've moved from your original concept.

Writing a letter to yourself is especially helpful if you're beginning to have anxieties about the book. Sometimes we try to suppress those anxieties, which only makes them worse. Anxiety turns to frustration and despair, and finally we abandon the whole project. If you can actually write down what bothers you about your subject, or your style, the answer to the problem often suggests itself. The act of turning our chaotic thoughts into orderly sentences seems to lead to much quicker and more satisfying solutions.

(Here's a slightly outrageous tip: *Don't respect the text.* Just because you've written something down doesn't mean it has a right to exist. If your internal editor can find a better way to say something, junk the original version and go with the new one. If you can't find a better way, and the passage really isn't good, junk it.)

In addition to these self-addressed letters, keep a daily log of your progress. Word processors' word-count functions are powerful encouragers. The log can give you a sense of accomplishment, especially on big projects, and can enable you to set realistic completion deadlines. For example, if you know you can write 500 words in an hour, and you write three hours a week, you can have a completed book manuscript of 75,000 words in 50 weeks. If you write ten hours a week, the manuscript will be complete in 15 weeks.

Compile a "project bible." This is a list of facts, names, and so on that you expect to be using for constant reference. If you have some important research findings you plan to use, put them in the bible along with their sources. The best format for this bible may be a looseleaf binder you can carry with you. (A word of caution: If your bible gets too big to carry easily, you're defeating its purpose.)

Opportunity: If you decide you "can't write" unless you're seated at your Gigabyte II computer with Mozart on the stereo and no one else in the house, you're just making life harder for yourself. Your routine will always contain "dead time" when you're away from home (or at least away from your workplace) with no other task at hand. You might be waiting in a doctor's office, on a bus, or trapped in a long, dull meeting. Use that dead time constructively by carrying a notebook in which you can record at least a few lines of a rough draft (or use your project bible). Or you might jot down some background notes about your project, or a self-editing idea that's just occurred to you. You can then use these when you're back at your desk producing finished text.

6

CORPORATE WEBWRITING

W hile the writing principles discussed in this book apply to all websites, writing text for corporate sites is different in some ways than writing for noncorporate sites. A corporate website reflects the consensus of a formal group — a company, a university, a government agency — about how it ought to present itself on the Web.

A commercial website for a retail outlet or webzine, for example, is more likely to reflect a single individual's vision, whether quirky or conformist. A corporate website is the result of a lot of meetings, and the input from a lot of sources may or may not help those who actually put the site together.

Admittedly, a corporate site may also reflect a single person's vision — if that person can sell it to the rest of the group creating the website. But in general, a corporate site is usually a compromise of some kind. If you are the webwriter for such a group, you face a host of largely political challenges in turning those compromises into good writing.

1. Challenges for Corporate Webwriters

Your first challenge as a corporate webwriter is to make your group understand what the Web can and cannot do, and how a website can further the group's interests. If you are also the group's webmaster, you presumably have the technical understanding of the requirements. You accept that part of your job is to educate your group about those requirements, and your group will usually take your word as final. Most of us, after all, defer to the HTML guru.

But it may be harder to explain to them the text requirements of a good site. You can explain how the writing on your group's site can exploit the Web's advantages while avoiding its pitfalls, but it may take a while to make your message understood. Most of us think *anyone can write*, so your colleagues are likely to express opinions on website content.

What if you're not the webmaster, and the group has called you in after accepting the technical suggestions of a nonwriter? Then you could have a problem, because the designer may have been concerned with technical questions of display, not with the principles of Orientation, Information, and Action.

As a webwriter you may face yet another tangle: your group may not have a consensus on what its own interests are and how the site will advance them. Very often, groups automatically adopt the old-fashioned communication model of the FedEx courier, delivering a message against all odds to a passive recipient whose only part in the process is to sign for the package. They aren't thinking about the "you" attitude discussed in Chapter 2, that good webwriting expresses ideas in terms of the reader's advantage. Too often, groups want to go onto the Web to talk only about how wonderful and important they are — not about how they can make themselves useful to their readers.

Marijke Rijsberman, a webwriter for a Silicon Valley consulting firm, put it this way in 1999:

> The company decides (and lots of companies are deciding the same thing) that [Web] content should be taken care of in the marketing department, as the gaggle of talent and experience most pertinent to the task. But the thing marketing departments typically do is take care of the message — what we want others to know about the company, whether or not they want to know about the company. The basic mindset is that of advertising: breaking into the awareness of people who are not looking for the information we want them to have.

> I suppose the model works for banner ads. But it does not work for other writing on the Web, which needs to recognize that people come looking for you. Of course, they don't come looking for ads, they come on the general assumption that the Web is an information-rich medium that may contain the answers to their questions.

> So yes, they may want to know about your company, but chances are that they really want information that's within the company's expertise and they want that information much more than the stuff you put in the corporate brochure.

When I asked her in 2006 if her opinion had changed, she replied:

In general, I think corporate webwriting has improved quite a bit. It has become clear that you can't just hook customers up to the feeding tubes as if they're geese being prepared to lay the foie gras. That kind of thing just doesn't lead to conversion.

But the general attitude is still very much alive internally in corporate environments. Internal communications departments are still in the business of making foie gras by traditional methods, with little regard for what employees really need to know to be productive or what it is like to be the recipient of the communications stream they envision.

What hasn't changed at all is that writing for the Web is only partially about writing well and engagingly. Figuring out what the user needs to know is still the bigger question. Jakob Nielsen argues that most corporate websites are not just failures, but are actively damaging to their creators' reputations. While he focuses on commercial sites, I think his findings are equally true for other group-sponsored sites.

The evidence Nielsen offers is pretty devastating. He cites one study of 15 big commercial websites in which users could find information only 42 percent of the time, even though they started from the home page each time. In another study, three out of five online shoppers had given up trying to find the item they wanted to buy. A third survey found that, out of 20 major sites, simple website organization principles (for example, "Is the site organized by user goals?") were observed only half the time.

"The odds are against any company that wants to put up a website," says Nielsen. "In my estimate, 90 percent of commercial websites have poor usability."

The problem, Nielsen argues, isn't even confined to "B2C" (business-to-consumer) sites. Well into the Web's second decade, he complains that "Business-to-business (B2B) sites are stuck in the 1990s in their attitude toward the user experience." His current tests show that users achieve only a 58 percent success rate in completing tasks on B2B sites. (Go to www.useit.com/alertbox/b2b.html.)

This poor success rate is all the more baffling because the decision makers are usually very focused on pleasing customers in ordinary marketplaces. Imagine a car dealership where you couldn't find a car (or a sales rep) on the lot, or a supermarket where you couldn't find the fresh produce or the checkout stands. Imagine a loan officer who bragged about the bank's assets, but never asked about your own financial needs.

Much of the problem with corporate websites is poor structure: visitors receive inadequate orientation, so they can't navigate to the information they want. And of course, if they don't have the information, they won't perform the action desired of them by the group running the site: they won't buy the product, join the party, apply for admission to the college.

But even when the site design is good, the quality of the writing may make the information unusable and the desired action unappealing to most readers.

2. Define Your Audience

A corporate site should reach a wide range of readers without trying to be all things to all people. A college site should address students (potential and enrolled), faculty, support staff, potential employees, and employers. A bank should address its own staff, its current and potential customers, and the business community. A municipal government site must address its residents and taxpayers, its staff, and potential investors.

All corporate sites should of course address the general public as well, but they will do that best by showing they know how to address their specific audiences.

In some cases, the site may invite particular readers to pages created just for them. Many companies, for example, list <u>Job Opportunities</u> as a link on their front page. Pages intended strictly for internal use by staff can be password protected.

Large organizations may be able to afford intensive research into their audiences, which of course will help them focus their website. In any case, it's important that a corporate site express a consistent tone that is appropriate to its intended audiences. (I discuss semantics and register in Chapter 8.) That means achieving a consensus within your organization both about your audience and about the best way to address it.

3. Corporate Webwriting Needs the "You" Attitude

In Chapter 1, I mentioned the FedEx communication model. Until fairly recently, most people — including writers — grew up learning to communicate in school and the workplace using the standard model, which assumes an active sender and a passive receiver for every message. The message itself is a lump of information that the receiver accepts like a downloaded file. The standard metaphors for this model are either postal ("Get the message?") or ballistic ("We're targeting the 18-to-35 demographic").

The technical term for this model is *instrumental*, because it works on the passive receiver like a crowbar or baseball bat, to create a specific desired response. The implicit message in this model is, "Do what I say."

The instrumental FedEx model works fine in media like print, radio, or TV. That's because the receiver has little or no chance to respond beyond a letter to the editor or a phone call to a talk-back line. Communication is effectively one-way.

But as I argued in Chapter 3, the Web really runs on a much more sophisticated and interactive model (also known as a *constructivist* model). In this model both sides constantly change roles — sending and receiving at virtually the same time, adapting each message in light of the last response. Both parties construe the meaning of the exchange, and it may end with both sides in unexpected territory, knowing things they didn't expect to know. The metaphor here is the conversation, and the implicit message is, "Is this what you want?"

Even the old FedEx model expects the receiver to sign for the package, or regurgitate the lecture, or vote as the spin doctor wishes. But it's still a vertical relationship between the boss and the bossed. On the Web, relationships are far more horizontal, and anyone who doesn't care to be bossed can escape with the click of a mouse.

And many Web sponsors — even the businesses that live or die by pleasing their customers — have still not understood this. The message on their sites is pure ego: We do this, we do that, we can make you happy, so make us happy by doing what we want you to do.

The Canadian scholar Northrop Frye once distinguished between *ego art* and *self art*. Ego art sees everyone as a worshipful audience for the ego's own splendor; the only purpose of the audience is to admire the perfect, unchangeable, yet always-insecure ego. Self art, by contrast, wants to provoke a response from other selves, to learn and change. The self, being secure, doesn't fear change — or challenge.

In business, good writing requires a "you" attitude that concentrates solely on the customer and the customer's needs. You don't even say: "We have a great deal for you, so do what we say" — you say: "You can take advantage of a great deal, if this is the deal you want." In other words, the constructivist, self-art model is interactive, a conversation with the reader/customer rather than an egomaniac's monologue.

So in the interactive medium of the Web, writers must keep their own egos offstage and engage the reader on terms of equality and shared interests. The webwriter expects to learn as well as teach, to move and to be moved. Such writing avoids fulsome, manipulative flattery. It sends a nonverbal message of respect and interest. A site that's slow to load and hard to navigate is an ego site. A quick-loading site with good navigation reflects a self-art site, considerate of readers. Webtext that's precious or bombastic may say a lot about the writer's big vocabulary, but it speaks much more loudly of the writer's big ego.

Even if we grew up as writers in the FedEx world of print on paper, we need to recognize that the old model doesn't work on the Web. Our readers may not know instrumentalism from constructivism, but they know when they're getting respect and when they're not. On the Web they enjoy a power of response that we ignore at our peril. But if we remember the "you" attitude and engage them in a genuine dialogue (as *The Cluetrain Manifesto* argues we should; see below), we will all profit from every online conversation.

 You can read *The Cluetrain Manifesto: The End of Business as Usual* at www.cluetrain.com. It's a thought-provoking challenge to everyone who wants to make money on the Web.

4. Too Many Webwriters Can Spoil the Site

Bureaucracies, whether corporate or governmental, can make life hard for the webwriter. Web designer Stephen Martin has seen what can happen when an organization allows too many people to do their own thing on its website:

> In the government world (and on many of the private sector sites I've worked on), the sites sometimes get compartmentalized by the group or department responsible for that area of the business (e.g., the Office of Management and Budget is responsible for the management and budget pages of the website). This often leads to a highly inconsistent site because there are so many different levels of experience and expertise working on the site. I've found that people also get very defensive about their writing (it's the "everyone's a writer" syndrome). They tend to write in long-winded flowery prose, or they are so terse as to be incoherent to all but those who are intimately familiar with the subject.
>
> The writing process is also subject to so many levels of approval that what you end up with looks nothing like what you started with. Imagine if everything you wrote went through a review by at least 12 different people (90 percent of whom are not writers or editors by trade).
>
> Trying to set guidelines and standards for content (even very broad standards) often leads to a backlash since different agencies and departments are very territorial and not about to give up what they see as their right to control "their section of the site." Most view my group

more as an Internet service provider than as the site's administrators and developers.

In other words, writing for a government website is often an exercise in futility.

While Martin's view reflects a real situation, don't let it discourage you. If you are writing for a corporate website, private or public, you may need to be a very good politician and a patient advocate. When you make your case for good, consistent writing on the site, follow the three webwriting principles mentioned in Chapter 2:

- Give your group the *orientation* it needs about the Web.

- Give it *information* it can use.

- Give it reasons to *act* in what it clearly understands are its own best interests.

Whether they're marketing government statistics, college courses, party memberships, or shareware, your colleagues need to understand how marketing works on the Web — and you're the person who has to sell them on that concept.

This doesn't mean sermonizing to these groups during committee meetings. More likely it will mean presenting them with a basic concept and approach toward the creation of the website that they can understand, that harmonizes with the group's communication style in other media, and that gives them the kind of jolt that visitors to the site should get.

Use Exercise 5 to help you analyze how others have designed their corporate websites.

Exercise 5
Analyzing Corporate Websites

On the web links page of the CD that came with this book, you'll find a number of corporate sites: companies, government agencies, charities, school districts, and universities. Select two or three comparable sites and write a brief review of each, using the criteria set out at the end of Chapter 3. Assume you are doing this on behalf of one of the organizations; your purpose is to identify the strengths and weaknesses of your own site in comparison with the sites run by your competitors.

1. Website: _____

   Review: _____

   _____

   _____

   _____

   _____

   _____

2. Website: _____

   Review: _____

   _____

   _____

   _____

   _____

   _____

3. Website: _____

   Review: _____

   _____

   _____

   _____

   _____

   _____

7

BLOGS, SELF-MARKETING, AND RÉSUMÉS

Blogs (web logs) transformed the Web in the first decade of the 21st century. In the 1990s, they were usually by and for technical experts — collections of links to sites dealing with particular computer applications or hardware. Familiar with HTML, bloggers could update their sites easily and often. The rest of us, struggling with early authoring tools such as Globetrotter and FrontPage, were glad just to get a page of content up with functioning links.

So the original blogs tended to reflect their authors' technical interests. As they rummaged around on the early Web, they found sites that interested them and created links to them. That made their own sites more interesting to others sharing the same interest.

As more people became comfortable with web authoring, blogs began to multiply. (BlogPulse, a tracking service, now estimates anywhere from 60,000 to 100,000 new blogs start up every day.) They also became more personal. New applications emerged that enabled bloggers to create professional-looking sites without knowing much HTML at all.

Blog topics multiplied too. By the year 2000, bloggers were offering the world their opinions on politics, knitting, movies, and every other subject. By the time I got into blogging in 2003, it was exploding thanks to services like Blogger, Movable Type, and TypePad.

The diversification of blogs since then has been dramatic. The Webby Awards recognize many types of blogs, ranging from the intensely personal to business to politics. Still, blogs tend to follow some basic conventions and fall into a few basic genres that often overlap. Writing in these new genres still relies on orientation, information, and action. But much depends on the genre you've chosen to write in.

1. The Personal Blog

The vast majority of blogs are the expression of individuals or small groups concerned with personal matters. They divide into *introvert* and *extrovert* blogs.

The introvert blog is all about the author's private life: personal joys and sorrows, intimate relationships, daily events, and so on. These may touch on larger issues, but only in passing. Examples are found all over the Web.

One of the striking aspects of this genre is the author's denigration of himself: the blog is purported to be "chaos," "random," "neurotic," and generally reflective of a failed life.

The content bears this out; posts are often highly self-critical, describing work not done, tests flunked, relationships failed. Even long gaps in the blogging record require mention and apology. Against this background, occasional highlights appear: a wonderful concert attended, a happy dinner with family, a new job.

The audience for such blogs consists, I would guess, of the author and a small number of friends, who will sometimes post encouraging responses. Introvert blogs tend to run long, long paragraphs, while most others tend to present short posts or at least long posts broken up into very short paragraphs.

I suspect that's because the nonintrovert blogs are aimed more at the reader, and the author realizes (instinctively or not) that long paragraphs are hard to read on a computer screen.

For the same reason, introvert blogs often have designs that make them hard to read — greyish text, for example, on a dark background, or white text on a black background. The readership is less important here than providing a blog that mirrors the author's feelings.

Extrovert blogs, by contrast, focus more on the blogger's surroundings: the neighborhood, the city, and the industry the blogger works in. A great example is Adventures of a Big White Guy Living in Hong Kong (http://bigwhiteguy.com), a Canadian expatriate's funny and opinionated view of life in his adopted city. Significantly, this site's layout is clean, bright, and inviting. (*The Diary of Samuel Pepys*, which is now posted day by day at www.pepysdiary.com, is the prototype of extrovert blogs.)

2. Job Blogs

Another genre is the job blog, in which the focus is on events at work. Depending on your interest in the job, this can be boring or fascinating. One of my favorites in this genre is Oh Jen Jen's It's a Zoo Out There (http://spacefan.blogspot.com).

Dr. Oh is a medical officer at Changi General Hospital in Singapore. In the spring of 2003 her blog was a mesmerizing narrative of the hospital's struggle to contain SARS — a struggle that cost the lives of several admired colleagues.

Dr. Oh's blog is clearly aimed at her colleagues, but during the height of the SARS outbreak in 2003 she was being read around the world. When SARS died out, she went back to routine emergency-room problems and talking about her favorite TV programs.

A hazard of the job blog, of course, is that it can cost you your job if you're indiscreet or your employers would prefer you not to talk in public about anything related to your work.

3. Specialist Blogs

The specialist blog, often a variant of the job blog, is closest in spirit and content to the early blogs of the 1990s. But the specialty may be far removed from computer applications.

Here the blogger is providing both new and old resources to a "community of interest." The community may be those interested in the career of a movie star, or new findings in archaeology, or the minute-by-minute progress of a World Cup soccer game.

A good example of a specialist blog is Nick Usborne's Web Copywriting (http://nickusborne.typepad.com). Usborne concentrates on how to write copy for online marketing. His advice is practical and to the point.

The specialist blogger assumes most readers are familiar with the shoptalk of the specialty, whether it's soccer or circuit design. This raises a writing problem: Should you avoid technical terms, or stop to explain them? Other specialists will be annoyed at constant interruptions to define what they already know. Newcomers to the field will be baffled by the jargon.

One possible compromise is to turn technical terms into links that take the reader to a glossary (or to create definitions that pop up when the reader's cursor rolls over such terms).

4. News Blogs

A news blog may be part of the online service of a print newspaper or a broadcaster's website. As such, it can both update news reports and create an archive for them. During the 2006 World Cup, many newspapers blogged the games, minute by minute. At the same time, they were running other blogs on their sites to cover news about technology, entertainment, business issues, travel, and education.

Some individuals and groups run news blogs as a way of putting scattered information in one place: World Cup coverage, for example (www.worldcupblog.org). Daily New Zealand News (http://newzealand.blogspot.com) summarizes events in New Zealand. And eMercedesBenz (www.emercedesbenz .com) reports news about Mercedes-Benz cars.

But you don't have to be a full-time professional journalist to run a news blog. My own site H5N1 (http://crofsblogs .typepad.com/h5n1/) gathers news about avian flu, and draws visitors from around the world.

I try to keep the text as short and clear as possible; many of my readers would be lost if I didn't. While I often analyze or comment on the stories I post, I prefer to let the stories speak for themselves, and to let readers draw their own conclusions.

The line between news and advocacy can often blur. You may link only to stories that support your view of the world, or your own comments on those stories may contain a strong bias. Your readers will always know where you stand, but they may also find you predictable and therefore not worth many repeat visits.

5. Advocacy Blogs

The sixth major category is the advocacy blog. Here the blogger is arguing the case for a group, movement, or philosophy: to promote Partners In Health (www.pih.org), or the Bush administration's efforts in the Middle East (www.littlegreen footballs.com/weblog/). Most corporate blogs are advocates for their organizations.

Some political advocacy blogs, especially in the United States, enjoy huge readerships and make money through the sale of online ads. If you dream of running a big, popular advocacy blog, do a very careful analysis of sites like InstaPundit (http://instapundit.com) or Daily Kos (www.dailykos.com). As well as studying the design, test the readability of the text on such sites.

6. Developing the Right Style for Your Blog

Of course these categories of blogs often overlap. A news blog may be specialized, like World Cup Blog. It may include personal comments and social observations, and may strongly advocate a particular agenda. Still, the genres tend to stand apart from one another and to appeal to distinct audiences.

The distinctions lie in part in the resources they offer. An introvert blog may link to sites selling the blogger's favorite CDs and books, or to the blogs of friends. An extrovert blog may link to such items, but will also link to governments, advocacy sites, or specialty sites related to the blogger's hobbies and recreational interests.

Each of these blog genres poses particular writing challenges. Introverts tend to write long paragraphs with very little "you" attitude. Extroverts may lack a consistent focus. Specialists may be so specialized and so fond of technical shoptalk that they exclude casual visitors.

Advocacy blogs are especially challenging for writers. As noted earlier, text on a computer screen works best with blunt assertions, not with long, careful arguments. This tends to encourage jolt-rich rhetoric, full of strong language and weak reasoning.

Advocacy bloggers will therefore find themselves talking mostly to the converted, with reference to adversaries only as a pretext for more strong language to jolt the converts.

Maybe some of the most introverted bloggers aren't interested in gaining more traffic, but everyone else is. Readers go to sites that they trust to give them accurate, reliable, and current information. Both style and content can help to build that trust, and therefore to build traffic. The three principles of webwriting are helpful.

6.1 Orientation

What your blog is about goes in the orientation section. Orientation can include the following:

- Title (avoid obscure or heavily ironic terms)

- Catchphrase (the "subtitle" that helps explain the blog's purpose)

- Main links (<u>About me</u>, <u>Email me</u>, and links with obvious relevance to the blog's main topic)

So if you're running a community news blog, your title and catchphrase might be:

Chesterton Newsletter

People, events, and issues in the Chesterton Valley

Consider how your readers might respond if instead you gave your blog a title and catchphrase such as:

Chesterton: The Land That Time Forgot

Your main links are important too. If your profile or "About Me" page is badly written, sarcastic, or simply uninformative, you can't expect readers' trust. If the links to other sites are obviously one-sided, readers will be skeptical: a link to the Communist Party of Canada, but not to the Chesterton municipal website, will not build confidence in your reliability as a source of information about Chesterton.

Titles and catchphrases can also build traffic. This is another reason for using simple, straightforward titles and catchphrases. If your blog followed the second example, you'd attract people Googling for information about Neanderthals or the Edgar Rice Burroughs novel *The Land That Time Forgot*. Neither group will care about your local political battles.

When I started my avian-flu blog, I chose H5N1 as the title and gave it a simple catchphrase: "News and resources about avian flu." Within a very few months, I discovered that a Google search for "H5N1" would put my site in the first three or four hits out of millions.

I suggest, then, that you choose your blog's title and catchphrase using clarity, brevity, and terms that your potential readers will type into Google when they want the kind of information you offer.

6.2 Information: What you want to tell your readers

The basic unit of blog prose is not the sentence or the paragraph, but the whole post. In effect, a post is like a miniature web page, usually with chunks of text and links to other sites. And like a web page, it should be able to stand on its own without reference to other pages. (Since blogs usually add new posts at the top, you can't even assume that your readers have seen your earlier posts.)

Each post, then, is like a chunk: a mini-essay. As such, it needs structure: an attention-grabbing hook, a clear exposition of your topic, perhaps a glimpse of something not obvious, and a closing "kicker" that wraps up the post.

As with most text to be read online, your posts should be short: short sentences, short paragraphs. When your content requires long, complex presentation, put it into a PDF or word-processed file — or into a video or podcast file.

If you're writing a personal blog for three friends, your style isn't important. You can ignore grammar, punctuation, and spelling — even coherence. Your friends will have the exformation to know what you're talking about. In other blogs, however, routine typos and lapses from Standard English will hurt your credibility.

But speed is the essence of blogging: you can say something quickly, and editing only slows you down. Who has time to write, print out, proofread, correct, and finally post something?

Blogging software itself can help. Most applications can supply at least spell checking. But you can do more than that.

For example, you may miss a typo or spelling error when you're composing. But as soon as you upload your post, the goof jumps out at you — just as if you were proofreading on paper. The change in format seems to make your text unfamiliar, so the errors are easy to spot. Then it's easy to go back, correct the error, and re-post it.

You can also compose a post as a draft, let it cool off, and then return to proofread it before posting. Writing in "draft" format also enables you to create a post, dig up an elusive fact, and then add the fact quickly before posting. If a reader spots an error you've missed, you can easily correct it.

6.3 Action: What you want your readers to do

Depending on the genre of your blog, you may want very little response from your readers, or a lot. A personal blog post invites comments or email from friends. A job blog or advocacy blog may invite readers to take all kinds of action: visit other sites, download documents, sign up for email lists or online forums, or join a professional association or political party.

Most of these actions require links. Some can appear in the post, or at the end of the post. Others can appear in lists displayed in columns alongside your posts. Remember that many readers are hesitant to click through to a site unless the link title, or its blurb, gives them a reason to.

Of course links can also include downloadable materials: PDFs, photos, podcasts and other audio files, and video clips. These can pose problems: if the file is too big or requires a particular application, some of your readers may not be able to access it. You can include a link to a site where the application can be downloaded.

Bloggers usually welcome comments, but this function has hazards. Some comments may be abusive or even defamatory. Others can be "comment spam," planted to attract your visitors to pornography or gambling sites.

Blog applications such as TypePad can protect your site by enabling you to delete unwelcome comments. You can even ban all comments from a given Internet Protocol (IP) address. (TypePad can also send you an email message whenever a comment appears on your site, so you can delete comments within minutes of their appearance.)

Keeping your blog free of nuisances can be time-consuming, but it's the price you pay for an interactive site — and if your site isn't interactive, it's just electronic graffiti.

7. Personal Sites for Self-Marketing

The personal site of the 1990s was like a slow-motion blog: a résumé for the "About Me" page, links to sites of interest, and archived material such as articles or graphics. For many of us, creating such a site was time-consuming, and updates were a lot of trouble. Once we had a personal site online, we tended to leave it alone.

In recent years, however, people have begun to adopt multiple personal sites: a seldom-changed archive plus often-changed blog sites.

Janice Wong, a Vancouver artist and writer, uses multiple sites to promote her art and her book, as well as reporting on current events. Start with her book site (http://c-h-o-w .blogspot.com) and you'll find a range of linked sites covering all her activities.

Chris Zawada, a graphic designer, does something similar: a portfolio site at www.chriszawada.com, plus a blog at www.banter.chriszawada.com.

Amy Gahran, a veteran webwriter, runs three blogs: Contentious (http://blog.contentious.com), The Right Conversation (www.rightconversation.com), and Mass of Contradictions (http://agahran.typepad.com/massofcontradictions/). Meanwhile, freelance writer Debbie Ridpath Ohi runs at least seven blogs; start with electricpenguin.com (www.electricpenguin .com) and follow the links.

Whatever the genre, much of the writing in the blog world is pretty bad. But I hope and believe that it will improve as bloggers become more comfortable with the medium and with the conventions of their preferred genres. Bloggers will try to emulate the writers they admire and to distance themselves from the bad writers.

In science fiction, Sturgeon's Law decrees that "Ninety percent of science fiction (and everything else) is junk." We can strive to reduce blog junk to a somewhat smaller percentage.

8. Résumés: Create a Portfolio on Your Site

Many job seekers turn up for a hiring interview with a portfolio that demonstrates their skills: reports written for previous employers, copies of ads they've written or designed, photos they've taken, letters of commendation, and awards. These can be an effective way of showing, not just telling, potential employers what you can do for them.

Your website, whether it's a single site or a cluster of sites, can serve as a portfolio that employers can consult even before they call you in for an interview. Consider some of the items you could include in your portfolio:

- Reference letters

- Awards

- Evaluations by previous employers

- Degrees and certificates

- Course descriptions or outlines (both for courses you've taken and courses you've taught)

- Writing samples: technical reports, business plans, proposals, ad copy, news releases, novels in progress, poetry

- Graphics samples: photos, video clips, line art

- News stories (whether by you or about you)

- Links to organizations or individuals

Some of these elements need careful thought. For example, do you want to include a scanned graphic of your college degree, or of an award you won as a freelance writer? They may document your achievements, but they may also imply you're too impressed with yourself. Are the writing samples really relevant to the job you're seeking, or just the kind of thing you enjoy doing for yourself?

If you provide an email link to a reference or previous employer, has that person given you permission to do so? After all, you're asking the person to go to the trouble of replying to queries about you — maybe a lot of them — and it's simple courtesy to check first to see if that's okay.

8.1 Provide useful services

Your portfolio should supply a benefit to potential employers even if they don't hire you. Maybe you're an accountant who has helped design a new spreadsheet; let your readers link to a demo version of the spreadsheet. Or, as a safety consultant, you developed emergency procedures for open-pit mines; archive your guidelines in easily downloadable form. You were a cook in a local steakhouse? Give us a great barbecue sauce recipe. (In all these examples, I assume you own the rights to what you're offering.)

If you've got the skills to be worth hiring, you know something useful that you can give away. By doing so, you build goodwill and likely reach potential employers who will never see your website — but they may well see a copy of your spreadsheet or guidelines or recipe that has been forwarded to them by someone else, and get in touch with you because they like what they've seen of your work. If they're really sensitive to the culture of the Web, they'll also recognize that out on the electronic frontier, pioneers lend a hand to one another — and since you've lent them a hand, they may be able to return the favor.

8.2 Make response easy

Your readers may well hop from page to page in your portfolio. If they like what they see, getting in touch with you should be as easy as you can make it. This is really a design question inspired by the "you" attitude. For example, each page should have a link titled something like <u>Email Me</u>. Click on it, and an email form pops up, pre-addressed to you. Or each page could include your name and address plus telephone number(s) and email address. That way, readers always know how to reach you.

Ease of access, by the way, sends another nonverbal message: I'm thinking of your needs and making life as easy as I can for you.

Another thoughtful touch: in addition to your online résumé, whether for scrolling or chunked, provide a PDF version that employers can print out for themselves for easy reference. Keep it simple and short — not more than three pages and preferably one or two. Normally such a version would not contain elaborate formatting, links, or other Web-dependent effects: just words and white space, laid out for easy readability.

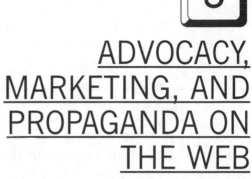

8

ADVOCACY, MARKETING, AND PROPAGANDA ON THE WEB

nformation is telling people how many motels there are in Chesterton; advocacy is persuading people to visit Chesterton because it will meet their needs; and marketing is persuading people to make a reservation at one of those motels. Many principles of advocacy and marketing in other media are the same on the Web. If your website's purpose is to promote a point of view or to sell an item or service, it's more likely to succeed if you keep in mind some basic principles of persuasion.

1. Semantics and Register

Many words have complex connotations. That is, they don't just refer to a particular thing or action or idea; they convey some kind of emotional aura as well. A restaurant may be a "fast-food joint" or a "bistro" — both offer quick service, but a bistro sounds classier. "Good eats" promises something different from "an elegant dining experience."

Semantics is the study of such meanings, and semanticists like to distinguish between *purr words* and *snarl words* — words whose connotations are either positive (at least to the speaker or writer) or negative. Such words may refer to the same thing, but carry very different meanings: *Certified General Accountant* and *bean counter*, for example, or *vintage automobile* and *beater*, or *educator* and *pedant*. In effect, purr words and snarl words convey our attitude toward whatever we're discussing.

As a persuasive webwriter, then, you should be aware of how your readers will respond to the words you choose. You should also consider the register to adopt in your text.

Register involves choosing words that reflect your understanding of the social situation and how the people involved see one another. When you write to a stranger, you address her as "Dear Ms. Robinson." That's the register of formal business writing, and Ms. Robinson accepts this term as a courtesy one stranger pays to another. Once you've become friends, you can write "Dear Helen," in a much less formal register. And what happens when you write "Dearest," or "Sweetest Helen"? Suddenly you're in a much more intimate register, and you'd better hope she doesn't write back, "Dear Mr. Smith"!

Register doesn't just convey the proper manners for the occasion. It can also determine the content of your message. When the president addresses the combined House and Senate, he doesn't say: "Folks, I am really ticked off about the way my political opponents are pulling my chain on the defense budget." He says: "Thank you, Mr. Speaker. My fellow Americans."

As a rule, the more people you're addressing at once, the more formal and abstract your message is likely to be. The fewer people you're addressing, the more informal and personal you can be.

What does that mean for you as a webwriter? Maybe thousands of people will visit your site; should you adopt an elevated public register, as if you were addressing a huge political rally? Or, since each reader arrives at your site as an individual, can you adopt an intimate personal register?

That depends to some extent on the nature of your site. If its purpose is to represent a serious organization — a bank, an environmental activist group, a political party's local branch — then the register should be serious also. Such organizations exist because of people's hopes and anxieties. No one wants to be even more anxious about the security of their savings or the direction their country is taking because of reading text with an inappropriate tone on an organization's website. This is why bankers and politicians tend to dress conservatively, unless they're trying for a "plain folks" image. They also speak conservatively and would expect cautious, correct language on their organization's website.

If the organization's purpose is fun, then the register ought to convey that. The website for a company that makes squirt guns or that markets backpacks to young world travelers is obviously going to be relaxed and lighthearted. It can afford to use slang or incorrect English, or even to exclude some people by using in-group terms.

Whether serious or fun, your site is trying to assure your readers that you speak their language, and that they can, therefore, trust you. If your use of semantics and register makes them feel like outsiders, they will be skeptical of your claims.

2. Three Elements of Persuasion

When you're writing to persuade your readers, you may have varied goals. If you want to reinforce readers' existing beliefs and values (also known as preaching to the choir), you have an easy job. We're always eager to hear that we're right. Changing your readers' beliefs is harder; it requires trust from your readers that you are concerned with their best interests. Hardest of all is getting people to act, even when you've been telling them they're right.

Bear in mind the major elements of good webwriting: orientation, information, and action. If you make it easy for your readers to respond, they will get in the habit of acting.

Short, powerful chunks of text can trigger strong emotions and willingness to act. In some ways webtext poses an ethical problem for the persuader: It's not suitable for careful, linear, logical argument, but it is excellent for jolt-rich slogans, captions, and unsupported assertions. Yet manipulating readers by appealing to their fears and insecurities is deeply disrespectful. If you're attempting to persuade your readers, it should be on the basis of appeals to their intelligence and maturity.

With that in mind, let's look at three aspects of persuasion as they operate on the Web.

2.1 Logical argument

Logical argument involves stating a proposition of some kind, along with supporting reasons. The reasons themselves must be supportable. So you might predict that the US population in 2050 will reach 394 million, with 20 million being women aged 80 or more. You could cite the US Bureau of the Census as your support for this argument, and perhaps that would be enough authority for most people.

If you think it is not enough for your particular audience, you would also have to describe the Census Bureau's methodology in reaching its prediction. Assuming that the methodology used generally accepted statistical projections (accepted because they've been accurate in the past), you could safely assert that you've made a logical argument for your population forecast.

2.2 Emotional appeal

By invoking ideas and images that stir our readers' feelings, we can gain attention that logical argument alone may not achieve. In some cases, we may not even care about the logic in an argument until something has dragged us emotionally into a confrontation with the issue. Only then will some people seek the logical argument to back up their strong feelings.

Again, the online advocate should be careful to avoid exploiting readers' anxieties. Appeals to emotion should be positive (invoking love, trust, friendship, or noble qualities like courage and honesty), rather than appealing to fear, hatred, and contempt.

This doesn't mean a positive emotional appeal is automatically a good argument. Love and courage are admirable, but they may serve detestable causes.

Unless you support a position because of strong emotions you don't want to examine, you probably came to your position by learning particular facts. These facts, in the context of your particular values, caused you to adopt the position you're now advocating. You may, therefore, find that facts, not loaded language, can inspire similar emotions in your readers.

2.3 Credibility

Using your readers' language, and registers they are comfortable with, can strongly enhance your credibility. But you also need to demonstrate a shared interest between you and your readers and convey sincerity through your tone and evident desire to help readers who visit your site. You should also have acceptable credentials — direct personal experience, specialized training, or at least a selection of respected and recognized authorities who can back up your assertions.

Relying on the "you" attitude can help your credibility by putting your arguments in terms of the reader's interest rather than your own. In its crudest form, this gives us the "crazy" retailer who's giving you a bargain that will probably bankrupt him or her. But if you can establish that you serve your own interests best by serving your readers' interests, you further enhance reader trust in you.

Some unscrupulous persuaders like to "stack the deck" by presenting only the information that makes them look good. A more effective way to establish credibility is to raise opposing arguments as serious objections — and then refute them. A frequently asked questions (FAQs) page — a page where such questions are cited and then answered — can also be an effective way to state your readers' reservations and show how you can demolish them.

3. Constructing Persuasive Webtext

Maybe you just want readers to accept your argument passively, but more likely you want them to act on it — to buy the product, vote for the candidate, or protest the outrage. As we've seen, webtext doesn't lend itself to long, cumulative, reasoned argument, and it doesn't have the emotionally overwhelming impact of a wide-screen movie with stereo sound. Given its limits, the medium can still stir readers to respond to your message if you remember the principles of orientation, information, and action.

3.1 Orientation

Your readers want to know where they are when they arrive at your site, and they also want to know where they stand in relation to you. If they feel you're on their side, they'll welcome your message more easily. You can establish rapport with readers by using the following techniques:

- **Show you understand your readers' concerns.** You can often do this by identifying something that your readers will recognize as a problem. The problem could be an oppressive government or the difficulty of saving money for a holiday.

- **Offer something that readers will agree with.** A generalization or striking slogan can make readers think they've found a kindred soul. It doesn't have to be a cliché, but it should state, as Alexander Pope observed, "what oft was thought, but ne'er so well expressed."

- **Ask for help.** Readers have the power to decide, to choose, to join — and you want readers to be aware of that power.

- **Suggest a benefit.** If your readers agree that a problem exists, offer a solution they will find beneficial: greater peace of mind, a clear conscience, a new experience.

3.2 Information

Your readers will want details about the facts backing up your argument. By providing further information, your argument becomes more legitimate and appealing to your readers. Try the following:

- Explain the benefit in some detail, using facts and figures if necessary.

- Surprise your reader with a new fact or perspective on a familiar subject; a reader presented with a new idea or understanding is open to persuasion. We trust people who are on our wavelength but ahead of us in understanding the issue.

- Discuss objections or drawbacks calmly, then rebut them and focus on positive arguments. Most of us have been fooled often enough to be suspicious of offers and arguments that are literally too good to be true, so readers will be suspicious even when they want to believe you.

3.3 Action

Make sure your argument ends with a strong call to action. The following tips can help encourage readers to take whatever action you would like them to take:

- **Show how action can solve the problem you've described.** You may give examples of earlier actions that got the desired results ("Last year's campaign paid for clean water supplies for six villages") or negative results based on failure to act ("Sixty-two children in the region died of cholera last year because of contaminated water").

- **Make the desired action clear and easy.** ("Just type in your name and email address." "Simply click on the Yes or No button to register your opinion instantly!" "Test your understanding with this quick quiz.") A complicated or time-consuming response will make your reader hesitate.

- **Stress the benefit of responding quickly.** Whether you're selling Alaska cruises or party memberships, delay can be fatal to your campaign. If appropriate, set a deadline: "Email us by September 15 and get a free consultation ($250 value)."

4. What's a Legitimate Appeal? What's Not?

You can legitimately appeal to —

- recognized authorities — people or organizations generally accepted as expert and reliable in their field

- scientific experiment and observation, producing results that others can duplicate

- logical deduction or extrapolation from established facts

- readers' emotions, but only when combined with other legitimate appeals

You're on shaky ground if you appeal to —

- anecdotal evidence ("My cousin was abducted by aliens")

- celebrity ("Tom Cruise opposes psychiatry")

- outside authorities trading on irrelevant expertise ("Joe Doakes, a nuclear physicist, says UFOs exist")

You're out of bounds if you appeal to —

- logical fallacies — mistakes in argument that sound logical but aren't (see Fallacy Files Weblog at www .fallacyfiles.org)

- hasty generalizations ("I lost a fortune in a Canadian casino"; "Canadians are a bunch of crooks")

- wishful thinking ("This stock is sure to go up")

- readers' prejudices ("Are you sick of the disaster in the public schools?")

- false authorities ("The document *The Protocols of the Elders of Zion* proves the Jews want to take over the world." This argument is still made by anti-Semites, though the *Protocols* was long ago proven to be a forgery by the Russian secret police, who plagiarized it from a French satire on Napoleon III published in the 1860s.)

5. Notes on Propaganda

When you write advocacy text, you're a propagandist — but that's not necessarily a bad thing. Propaganda tries to influence large numbers of people, using the mass media as its chief vehicles: print, film, TV, and radio. Millions of websites are now propaganda vehicles also. Like any other form of persuasion, a website appeals to both reason and emotion. However, it tends to rely more heavily on emotional appeals since it must reach such a large and varied audience.

As an honest advocate, you should be aware of what propaganda can and cannot do, and what it should and should not do. That means understanding the types of propaganda, the attitudes that it relies on, and the ways that propaganda techniques may be abused.

6. Major Types of Propaganda

- **Social:** Develops or strengthens attitudes and beliefs over the long term, especially in news broadcasts, entertainment, sports. Example: reports on a string of government scandals that make the ruling party look corrupt and incompetent.

- **Shock:** Mobilizes an audience over a short time, using attitudes developed by social propaganda. Example: TV election ads attacking government corruption and incompetence. The shock is not intended to scandalize or outrage, but to motivate the audience to act.

- **Black:** Propaganda that is supposedly a message from one side of a conflict, but is in fact originating from the opposing side. It is used to distort the message, or to misrepresent or embarrass the enemy. Sometimes one side's own propaganda can inadvertently serve the same purpose by making unbelievable assertions. For example, in the spring of 2003, the Iraqi ministry of information claimed Iraq was defeating the Americans. Americans simply laughed at the claims.

- **Silent:** Suppresses or ignores inconvenient or damaging information. Examples: covering up a politician's misbehavior (Watergate); government silence about its involvement in illegal activities (Iran-Contra). Exposure of silent propaganda may result in both social-propaganda and shock-propaganda campaigns.

7. Propaganda Myths

In propaganda, a myth is an assertion about reality that may or may not be true, but which many of us strongly believe. Myths are often unprovable because they are outside the realm of verifiable fact, but millions of people have killed and been killed to uphold such unprovable beliefs. Here are some typical myths that, true or not, have inspired much modern propaganda:

- **Progress:** Everything's getting better; tomorrow will be better than today; yesterday was awful. Our supporters are advanced and progressive; our enemies are dinosaurs and cavemen.

- **The Last Judgment:** We'll pay for our crimes/errors some day. So we should stop oppressing people, exploiting women, damaging the environment, running up the deficit.

- **Racial Superiority:** Some races are smarter, nicer, sexier, more athletic, more law-abiding than others.

- **The Subhuman Enemy:** Our enemies are bestial and vicious and deserve no better treatment than animals. So cops are "pigs" and anticommunists are "running dogs."

- **The Scapegoat:** Our problems are all due to the corporations, or the unions, or the immigrants. So we don't have to examine our own failings.

- **National Superiority/Inferiority:** We Canadians are just like the Americans, only nicer. Swedes can't play rock 'em sock 'em hockey.

- **The Real Man:** A real man enlists for combat, wears the pants in his family, and doesn't eat quiche or write poems.

- **The Real Woman:** A real woman is attractive, fertile, enjoys the fine arts, and sacrifices herself for her husband and children.

- **The Conspiracy:** The CIA/Jewish bankers/neoconservatives are causing all the trouble in the world.

- **The Underdog:** Whoever is smaller or weaker in a dispute is probably in the right.

- **The Martyr:** Our leader/companion vindicated our cause by dying for it.

- **The Great Leader:** Our leader personally embodies all our national/cultural/racial virtues.

8. Basic Propaganda Devices

Used properly, these devices can sometimes form part of rational debate. For example, the testimonial device can bring real authorities into the argument, or present what ordinary people think. A majority of citizens may support a given policy, and thereby legitimize that policy.

Most people who use these devices, however, only want to trigger strong emotions — not logical thought — in the target audience:

- **Name Calling:** "You dirty fascist/communist/racist/sexist!"

- **Glittering Generalities:** "Liberty, equality, fraternity"; "Peace, order, and good government." Emotional but abstract words that make good slogans but poor policy.

- **Transfer:** Swastika, stars and stripes, maple leaf — powerful graphic symbols associated with something the propagandist wants people to support or oppose. Flag-burning exploits the transfer device by symbolically destroying the enemy.

- **Testimonial:** Support for an idea based on authority ("Professor Smith agrees"), celebrity ("Tom Hanks agrees"), plain folks ("Joe Doakes agrees").

- **Card Stacking:** One-sided argument: "We have 85 percent full employment!" Closely related to silent propaganda.

- **Bandwagon:** Many supporters make an idea valid; few supporters make an idea invalid. "A *growing* number of concerned Canadians"; "A *small but vocal* gang of troublemakers ... "

- **Identity Threat:** "Our opponents are a menace to our nation/society/class/group/sexual orientation." This is one of the most powerful propaganda devices, used in election campaigns (which are shock propaganda) and in much social propaganda (everything from comic strips to news reports).

- **Triumph:** "We've done a great job, so re-elect us."

- **Outrage:** "They've done an awful job, so throw the bums out."

The paradoxes of propaganda

- Much propaganda is personally and socially constructive. (It encourages us to drive safely, treat others kindly, and obey the law.)

- Propaganda works best on the converted. (They always want more confirmation that they're right.)

- Propaganda works best on educated people. (People don't care about what they don't know about; university graduates think they can change the world.)

- Truth is the best propaganda; next best is the half-truth; and silence is usually preferable to an outright lie. (If they catch you lying, they stop believing you.)

- Enemy propaganda can be excellent propaganda for one's own side. ("How can those idiots believe such claptrap!")

- Straight news or entertainment can conceal propaganda (especially social propaganda trying to confirm or change social attitudes).

- Propaganda that seems to argue against its own self-interest is more credible. ("We teachers are overpaid. You should cut our salaries or demand more work from us.")

- When propaganda is really good, it can make people act against their own beliefs. ("War is awful, but Saddam Hussein was a monster we had to stop"; "I don't agree with either candidate, but I'll hold my nose and vote for the lesser of two evils.")

9. Analyzing Advocacy Websites

Countless websites and blogs are arguing for or against something. If you are writing for such a site, it can be helpful to review and critique a wide range of advocacy sites. But this can be challenging.

If you visit a site that supports the same things you do, it's easy to admire and imitate it. However, you don't want to preach to the proverbial choir — you want to make converts and win new supporters.

So look at both the competition and the opposition, and remember the "you" attitude. Put yourself in the shoes of the people who may visit such sites. Are they looking for reassurance or a whole new point of view? Are they looking for a way to act effectively about a problem or just trying to inform themselves?

On the CD that came with this book, you'll find links to a wide range of advocacy sites, from political parties to humanitarian nongovernmental organizations to religious groups. Assess such sites in the light of the kinds of appeals they make, and the kinds of propaganda myths they employ. How effective do they appear to be? Do they have a lot of traffic — and can you trust their traffic statistics? Do visitors post many comments? Do such comments reflect the kinds of people you would like to attract to your site?

Propaganda has a bad reputation because so many propagandists understand their audiences but have no respect for them. Such propaganda relies on the instrumental model — it wants to manipulate the audience into obeying the command "Do what I say!"

If you are more interested in launching a conversation with your audience, raising issues, and expecting to learn something yourself, then the interactive communication model of the Web can serve you well. But not all who write advocacy on the Web have understood that.

9

FREQUENTLY ASKED QUESTIONS

he Web is already home to many flourishing genres, from muckraking journalism to erotica to avant-garde fiction. Each of these genres probably deserves a how-to book of its own, and will doubtless get it before long. The theory of such forms of webwriting will emerge from actual practice as thousands of writers experiment to see what works and what doesn't, right on the Web itself.

While looking forward to the appearance of such books, let's try to deal with some basic questions and point interested readers to the ongoing discussions that are attempting to answer them.

153

1. Can I make money as a freelance writer on the Web?

Some can, and many are trying. In some cases, freelancers are simply using the Web as a faster way to pitch story ideas to editors of print-based periodicals. In the mid-1990s, this often worked well because email was still a relative novelty and editors paid more attention to electronic queries. Since then, the flood of queries has caused many editors to ignore electronic queries on principle.

The number of paying online markets is still very small. I suggest you research those markets carefully; one place to start is on this book's blog, http://crofsblogs.typepad.com, and visiting the sites of the online magazines listed there. You may find some that would welcome your kind of writing.

2. Can I teach webwriting?

Someone in your company or school has to be able to write Web content besides you. So if you're the most experienced webwriter around, chances are you'll end up teaching your colleagues or students how to write for the Web.

You can teach webwriting successfully — especially if you set up your course or workshop so that your students really teach themselves. The principles that make a good website are also the principles that make a good course.

Start with the key question you ask when creating a website: Who is your audience? How narrowly can you define it? Do you want to reach nuclear physicists, cancer patients, hiphop fans?

And who, therefore, are your students? Are they colleagues in your company or students just passing through your classroom? Why do they want to learn webwriting — to make themselves more employable in future, or to hang on to a job right now? Can they choose the kind of website they're creating, or must they accept an existing site as their workspace?

The answers to those questions will help determine both your course content and the style and tone in which you express it. You'll have to take your students' strengths and weaknesses as your starting point.

Any good website does the same thing: its purpose is to serve the user, not flatter the creator. If your students don't know technical terms, then you'll have to avoid them (or define them clearly when you must use them). If they know XML but can't spell *extensible*, then you'll have to spend time on correct spelling.

Coming out of a print-oriented business or school culture, your students will want to write long texts — but you know hypertext often works best in short, stand-alone chunks of 100 words or less. Students know when they're dealing with a good or bad site, but they may have trouble explaining why. And they may forget that this is an interactive medium that succeeds only when the user responds to the information on the site.

Here are six techniques to help your students teach themselves webwriting:

1. Tell your students to write a 500-word essay. After you've returned it with your comments and corrections, announce their second assignment: To cut the first essay by 50 percent or more ... and still have it be cohesive and make sense.

   Students are used to padding their essays with BS, but now the prize will go to the leanest, cleanest prose they can bring out of the first essay. You'll be amazed at how quickly and brutally they can cut their own work, and yours. (By the way, the first draft of this section was 1,100 words long; it's now 795 words.)

2. Ask them to cut again until they get below that 100-word maximum for a chunk. They can't? Can they break the text into two chunks?

3. Further editing assignments, especially adapting long print text to the Web, will hone their skills and train them to find natural breaks between passages that can stand alone on the Web if need be.

4. Ask your students to write website reviews. Let them use their own standards, or apply those of a usability wizard such as Jakob Nielsen. By writing about those sites, your students will have to articulate their opinions, not just say: "This sucks, that doesn't."

5. Ask for detailed proposals for their own sites: purpose, intended audience, content … even the hours they estimate it will take them to write their Web content. Then they can rough out a site map or outline, without having to improvise or hope for sudden inspiration.

6. Put students' draft webtext up on a chalkboard or overhead transparency so everyone can see it — and rip it apart. Is it short? Usable? Understandable? Does it invite response?

No doubt you'll want to do much more, but these assignments and activities have been the core of my own webwriting course, and they've worked.

What's more, they've worked in a regular classroom, not in a computer lab. Put students in front of networked computers, and they're all over the planet before you can give them the first URL you want them to find. Use a single computer and a projector in a darkened classroom, and they fall asleep. If they're spending the rest of their day staring at a monitor, they'll be grateful not to have to do so in your class.

Plan on something else important: Your students won't just teach themselves. They'll teach *you* a lot about this medium and the way words work in it. Interactivity isn't just on site — it'll happen in your class as well. And you'll go on learning something new every time you teach how to write for the Web.

3. Can I create my own e-zine?

Sure. The line is blurring between the original e-zines such as *Salon*, and today's multiple-author blogs. Both genres are trying to attract large audiences and thereby attract advertising.

Some online magazines (and blogs) solicit advertisers directly, charging a small sum for each reader who lands on a page with the ad — or who clicks through the ad to the advertiser's own site. Others make a deal with Google or other agencies, which provide topic-related ads. You may have to choose your words carefully; mention that you're depressed about the state of the world, and you could be advertising online antidepressants!

The question is whether your e-zine or blog will attract enough readers to interest advertisers. If it does, advertising will help pay the costs of the e-zine and maybe even pay you something. If it doesn't, your e-zine will be just a hobby.

As with any other form of self-publishing, you should consider whether you're a writer, a businessperson, or both. If you're primarily a writer, looking after the business end of running an e-zine will be time taken away from what you really enjoy doing. If you enjoy both writing and business, an e-zine could be an ideal way to combine your interests.

4. Can I write hypertext fiction for the Web?

Yes, but it's a highly demanding form in which no one has more than a few years' experience. If you are interested in exploring this genre, the best place to start is probably the Eastgate Systems home page (www.eastgate.com).

Eastgate has been actively promoting hypertext fiction since the late 1980s, and has published pioneering work in the field. Its site also supplies links to many other hypertext-fiction resources on the Web.

5. Can I ensure that my blog is read only by people I want to read it?

I'll let Debbie Ridpath Ohi, an experienced online writer, answer this one:

> I've always been somewhat baffled by people who post something negative about a particular person or company on their blogs and then get upset when the injured party finds out about it. Yes, you may have the site password-protected, use a pen name, and be careful about where you post the URL. But there is still no guarantee that your site will remain private.
>
> I always take the policy that anything I post online about anyone will eventually reach that person's ears. In cases of password-protected sites and blogs written under pen names, remember that it takes only one leak to open your site up to the rest of the world.
>
> You may reassure yourself that you could always edit or remove entries later on if necessary, but don't forget that there are archiving search

engines out there that could still make it possible for people to look at older versions of your blog even if you decide to delete the whole site.

6. Can I copyright my webwriting?

Yes, but the issues surrounding intellectual property are complex and rapidly changing.

For example, some writers have found that when they sell an article to a print magazine, they've also unwittingly given away the electronic rights in perpetuity. The publishers can put the articles up on their magazine's website and use them to attract other readers, who in turn attract advertisers, who pay the publishers. But the publishers don't have to split that income with the writers, because the publishers hold the rights to the articles.

Many writers' organizations are fighting this practice, and freelancers are trying to get their publishers to state in advance exactly what rights they are buying. It will doubtless remain a vexing problem for years to come, especially in a medium where copying is so easy and copyright enforcement so difficult.

Meanwhile, you may find yourself violating someone else's copyright — knowingly or otherwise — by pasting parts of a Web-published document into your own work. It's always a good idea to get permission from the copyright holder before you use even a graphic from someone else's site. You may find that the holder of the copyright will grant permission to copy in return for a link on your site to the original item.

The following websites should give you a general sense of how copyright affects you and your work:

- Electronic Frontier Foundation (an important site for many other resources as well): www.eff.org/IP/

- Computer Professionals for Social Responsibility: Intellectual Property: www.cpsr.org/issues/ip/

- Digital Future Coalition: www.dfc.org

- International Federation of Library Associations and Institutions: Copyright and Intellectual Property: www.ifla.org/II/cpyright.htm

- World Intellectual Property Organization: www.wipo.int

- US Copyright Office: www.copyright.gov

- American Society of Journalists and Authors: Copyright Registration: www.asja.org/pubtips/copyrite.php

- Creative Commons: http://creativecommons.org

7. How do I cite Web sources in scholarly writing?

The Web is becoming an indispensable research tool (and, alas, a resource for plagiarists), but it's happened so fast that authorities are still developing standard forms of citation.

Generally accepted types of citations follow this basic format:

> Author. "Article Title." *Periodical/Book/Website Title*. Date given on web page. Date accessed by reader. URL.

The author's name appears with the last name first (if the item has more than one author, subsequent authors appear with first name first). The title of the article appears in quotation marks, with a period inside the close quotation. The name of the periodical, website, or book appears with the main words capitalized and the whole title italicized or underlined. The date of the web page is given as well as the date you accessed it, since of course the page may well have changed since you did so.

For example:

Kilian, Crawford. "The Visions of Ji Won Park." *The Tyee.* May 29, 2006. Accessed August 11, 2006. http://thetyee.ca/Photo/2006/05/29/JiWon/

For more detailed guidelines, consult these online resources:

- Research and Documentation Online: http://dianahacker .com/resdoc/

- Columbia Guide to Online Style: www.columbia.edu/ cu/cup/cgos/idx_basic.html

- Electronic Citation Guides (University of Texas at El Paso Library): http://libraryweb.utep.edu/db/citing.cfm

- Journalism Resources: Guide to Citation Style Guides: http://bailiwick.lib.uiowa.edu/journalism/cite.html

8. Can a website enhance a book on paper?

Yes. Most new textbooks offer websites as a way to update and expand their print content. In fact, it's now unusual for a textbook not to have a website with additional resources.

Other kinds of books will no doubt follow this development. In nonfiction, websites enable content to stay current without producing a whole new print edition. (This book has such a site — my blog Writing for the Web, at http://crofs blogs.typepad.com)

In fiction (and nonfiction as well, no doubt), websites give readers an opportunity to respond directly to the author and publisher. Authors are running their own blogs to promote their books and report on their current works in progress.

Many publishers are already posting excerpts from print books on their sites as a way to stir up interest in the book. This follows a practice of some paperback publishing houses, which may include an excerpt from a forthcoming book in the back of another novel — like the Coming Attractions at a movie.

Some publishers are even putting whole manuscripts online. Readers can either read the whole book onscreen (often paying to do so), or pay for a custom-printed copy. Authors themselves are divided on the value of such schemes.

9. Can I use a website to enhance the courses I'm teaching?

Yes, but don't expect it to transform the way you teach. I've been running blogs for my courses for several years. The students like having a place where they can download an extra copy of the course outline or yesterday's handout. They may use some of the links you provide, and they may enjoy the class photos you upload to the site.

However, it's usually up to the instructor to keep the blog running. So that means more work for you. Students may decide to skip a class if they know the handouts will soon be available online.

Making students coauthors of the blog may encourage other students to become more active on it, but they already have a lot to do and not much spare time.

Bear in mind also that not all your students may have easy access to computers — so a convenience for some students means an extra trip to a public computer in the school library or an Internet café for others. (I've created experimental blogs for classes in China, and lack of access to networked computers is a major problem there.)

To gain a sense of how to use blogs in courses, visit my site Prototype (http://crofsblogs.typepad.com/prototype/). I don't post to it often, but the information and links there may be helpful.

10. How can I balance keywords that will bring traffic to my site with the need to inform or sell to users once they arrive at the page?

This can be a problem. It used to be that if designers buried dozens of "invisible" keywords at the top of a home page, that site would get lots of traffic. But search engines are smarter than they used to be; today such pages are likely to be ignored, and a good thing too.

It helps to bring traffic to your site if you title your site with a word or phrase your audience is likely to use. That's why I called my flu blog "H5N1: News and resources about avian flu." Inevitably, I use *H5N1* and *avian flu* and *bird flu* in most of my posts. Even so, I was surprised to find that within a few months, Google put my site on the first page of search results. In the summer of 2006, a basic Google search for "H5N1" put it at number two out of 18,100,000 hits. (The number-one hit is H5N1 in Wikipedia.)

For more detailed advice, visit SuccessWorks, www.searchenginewriting.com, a site that focuses on just this issue.

11. How can writers and graphic designers work together?

I'll let graphic designer Chris Zawada answer this one:

The best way writers can work with designers is essentially just that ... working together. Most of the time the designer and writer will work in separate bubbles: the writer will write a block of text which he or she feels works best for the client's needs ... and separately the designer will design and drop in the amount of "lorem ipsum" text that he or she feels works best esthetically with the design.

Unfortunately, more often than not the final copy will be either too long or too short for the space the designer allotted. When the two parties can work together and bounce ideas off each other, and keep each other up to speed with design and copy, this problem can easily be averted.

AFTERWORD

I n a book about interactive writing, no one has the last word — least of all the author. Whether you've read this book in linear fashion or hopped around in it as if it were hypertext, you've been engaged in some kind of dialogue with it. Maybe you scribbled in the margins, or threw the book across the room. Maybe you changed your websites, or perhaps you left them exactly as they were to show how unimpressed you were with my argument.

But the Web is designed for dialogue as print is not. If you have questions, comments, objections, or worries about what you've read here, by all means let me know. You can reach me at:

crof@shaw.ca

And you can also reach me through my blogs:

Writing for the Web
http://crofsblogs.typepad.com

Writing Fiction
http://crofsblogs.typepad.com/fiction/

Ask the English Teacher
http://crofsblogs.typepad.com/english/

Prototype
http://crofsblogs.typepad.com/prototype/

H5N1
http://crofsblogs.typepad.com/h5n1/

APPENDIX

1

DICTION:
CHOOSE YOUR
WORDS
CAREFULLY

D iction refers to the choice of words used to express an idea. Here are some words that may cause confusion if you choose them for the wrong purpose. Sometimes they sound like the term you want, or they've been misused so constantly that they sound right to you.

- *adverse*: harmful, negative. Some antibiotics cause adverse reactions in patients.

- *averse*: reluctant, opposed. She was averse to confronting her boss about the problem.

- *affect* (verb): to influence. This news will badly affect our share prices.

- *effect* (noun): result. This news had a bad effect on our share prices.

- *aggravate*: make worse. This news will only aggravate our image in the market.

- *irritate*: annoy. The board members were irritated by the bad news.

- *alot*: incorrect form of *a lot*. A lot of people make this mistake.

- *allot*: to divide or apportion. We can allot 50 seats on a first-come basis.

- *allude to*: suggest without naming. He alluded to his earlier successes.

- *refer to*: name directly. She referred to her best-selling Harry Potter books.

- *alright*: incorrect form of *all right*.

- *ambiguous*: having two or more meanings. *Biweekly* is ambiguous because it could mean twice a week or once every two weeks.

- *ambivalent*: having mixed or conflicting feelings. I feel ambivalent about challenging him on this issue.

- *among*: refers to three or more. The prize money was divided among the four winners.

- *between*: refers to two. The prize money was divided between the two winners.

- *amount*: refers to uncountable items. Feeding an army requires a large amount of flour.

- *number*: refers to countable plural items. Feeding an army requires a large number of trained cooks.

- *apparently*: presumably, by appearances. Since he didn't answer the door, he's apparently left the house.

- *obviously*: without doubt, plainly. Since we've searched the house, he's obviously left.

- *assume*: accept as a premise in an argument. Let's assume we bring in a flat tax.

- *presume*: take for granted. I presume his government will bring in a flat tax.

- *assure*: to promise. We can assure you of a great stay in our B&B.

- *ensure*: to make certain. You can ensure success by careful planning.

- *insure*: to guarantee against loss. Here's how to insure all your valuables with one policy.

- *canvas*: coarse cloth. The canvas sails were in shreds.

- *canvass*: to seek support. She will canvass the delegates on behalf of her candidate.

- *cement*: component of concrete; binding agent. Let's cement our agreement with a toast!

- *concrete*: hard material used for construction. The concrete overpass collapsed without warning.

- *censor*: to delete or suppress sensitive or dangerous information. The government censored reports from the battlefield.

- *censure*: to condemn or disapprove. The protestors censured the government's suppression of the news.

- *cite*: quote or summon. I can cite several authorities. They were cited for speeding.

- *sight*: to see or take aim. Dave Johnson sighted a UFO on April 2.

- *site*: location; also short form for "website." This is a good site for links to Malaysian businesses.

- *client*: user of the services of a business or of a non-medical professional. As a client of Textor, you can expect the best in Web design.

- *customer*: person who buys from a store or business. As a customer of Self-Counsel Press, you're assured of prompt deliveries.

- *climax*: highest point, turning point in a story. The book's climax is deeply shocking.

- *crescendo*: growing in loudness or intensity. The crescendo of applause ended with a standing ovation.

- *complement*: to complete, or a total. This tie will complement your suit very well. The ship carries a complement of 32 crew members.

- *compliment*: to praise. I must compliment you on that elegant tie.

- *compose*: make or create. This committee is composed of six industry representatives.

- *comprise*: include or embrace. This committee comprises six industry representatives. (Note: Never say *comprised of*.)

- *convince*: to win an argument through appeals to logic and intellect. The experiment convinced even the skeptics.

- *persuade*: to win an argument through appeals to emotion. His tears and choked voice persuaded her of his sincerity.

- *country*: the territory of a nation. Canada is a very large country.

- *nation*: the people of a country. Canadians are a largely peaceable nation.

- *desert*: a desolate region; to abandon; or something deserved. The rocky desert stretched to the horizon. He deserted his companions. The king praised each knight according to his desert.

- *dessert*: a sweet. We had key lime pie for dessert.

- *different from*: used before a noun or pronoun. Taxco is different from Cuernavaca.

- *different than*: used before a clause. Taxco was different than I had expected.

- *disinterested*: impartial, neutral. A disinterested arbitrator resolved the dispute.

- *uninterested*: not interested. The arbitrator was uninterested in minor issues.

- *effective*: having a desired result; coming into operation. The new policy, effective on Monday, should be an improvement.

- *effectual*: performing as desired. Her arguments were effectual in winning the debate.

- *every day*: each day. We record the air temperature four times every day.

- *everyday*: routine. Recording air temperature is an everyday activity for us.

- *fewer*: used with countable plural items. We've had fewer hits on our site this month than last month.

- *less*: used with uncountable singular items. We have less traffic on our site this month than last month.

- *healthful*: promoting good health. Vegetables form part of a healthful diet.

- *healthy*: in good health. She remained healthy and alert well into her 90s.

- *hoard*: a supply of something. We have a hoard of canned goods in the basement.

- *horde*: a large number of people. A horde of bargain hunters swarmed into the shop.

- *home in on*: approach a desired goal. The pilot homed in on the radio beacon's signal.

- *hone in on*: incorrect but widespread usage; *hone* means sharpen, so the expression is meaningless.

- *imply*: suggest, hint. I don't mean to imply that the mistake was deliberate.

- *infer*: conclude, deduce. From the evidence, we can infer that the mistake was accidental.

- *incidence*: rate of occurrence. The incidence of drug-resistant tuberculosis is growing rapidly.

- *incident*: event. We've all learned from this unfortunate incident.

- *irregardless*: incorrect or humorous corruption of *regardless*.

- *its*: belonging to it. The committee has a lot on its agenda.

- *it's*: contraction of *it is* or *it has*. It's going to be a long meeting. It's been raining all afternoon. (By the way, *its'* is not a word at all.)

- *lead* (verb): present tense. She can lead us to the crash site.

- *led* (verb): past tense. She led us to the crash site. (Don't confuse this with lead, the metal!)

- *loath*: reluctant, averse. He was loath to confront the problem.

- *loathe*: detest, hate. He loathes his adversaries.

- *majority*: More than 50 percent of a countable group. The majority of the delegates supported the motion.

- *most*: More than half of an uncountable item. We spent most of the afternoon snorkeling over the reef.

- *moral*: having to do with good and evil. We faced a painful moral decision.

- *morale*: group spirit. Morale in the office sank when we heard the news.

- *perquisite*: a special privilege (perk). A new car is one of the perquisites of the job.

- *prerequisite*: a condition or requirement. A BA is a prerequisite for admission to our program.

- *principal*: first or most important. My principal motive was to create a simple, elegant website.

- *principle*: rule or idea. We support the principle of free speech on the Web.

- *proponent*: advocate. She is a proponent of free speech on the Web.

- *protagonist*: central character in a story. Ged is the protagonist of Ursula K. Le Guin's Earthsea novels.

- *reign*: time of a monarch's rule. England prospered during the reign of Elizabeth I.

- *rein*: harness or control. Our teacher gave us free rein in the library.

- *seasonable*: appropriate to the season. Rainfall has been seasonable this summer.

- *seasonal*: pertaining to the season. We've broken the seasonal record for rain this summer.

- *toe the line*: conform. The soldiers formed even ranks by toeing the line.

- *tow the line*: incorrect usage, a misspelling of *toe the line*.

- *waive*: give up. You can waive your right to a jury trial.

- *wave*: move back and forth. Wave good-bye to your hard-won rights!

In many of these cases, the difference between using the correct term and the incorrect one can be a spelling error that the spell checker on your computer will miss. That's also true of many other words: *to, two,* and *too; there, their,* and *they're; coarse* and *course.* Chances are you already know the words you have trouble with, so check them repeatedly against a dictionary until you're sure you're using them correctly.

2

COMMON ABBREVIATIONS

Business Abbreviations

acct or a/c	account
AG	Aktiengesellschaft, joint stock company (German)
ARM	adjustable rate mortgage
ASAP	as soon as possible
assn./assoc.	association
ATM	automatic teller machine
atty.	attorney
bal.	balance
Bcc.	blind carbon copy
b.l., b/l, B/L	bill of lading
CA	chartered accountant (Canadian designation)

CEO	chief executive officer
CFO	chief financial officer
CGA	certified general accountant (Canadian designation)
CIO	chief information officer
c/o	care of
CPS	certified professional secretary
ctn.	carton
CY	calendar year
cc, Cc	carbon copy
Cia.	compañía, company (Spanish)
Cie.	compagnie, company (French)
co., Co.	company
c.o.d.	cash (paid) on delivery
CPA	certified public accountant (US designation)
dba	doing business as
dis.	discount
dtd.	dated
ea.	each
EEO	equal employment opportunity
EOM	end of month
Ext., ext.	telephone extension (for example, Ext. 337)
FAX, fax	facsimile copy
FOB, f.o.b.	free on board (delivered without charge to buyer)
frt.	freight
fwd.	forward
FY	fiscal year
FYI	for your information

GATS	General Agreement on Trade in Services
GATT	General Agreement on Tariffs and Trade
GDP	gross domestic product
G.M.	general manager
GmbH	Gesellschaft mit beschränkter Haftung (German for limited liability company)
GNP	gross national product
hdlg.	handling
HR	human resources
HRD	human resources department
ID	identification
inc., Inc.	incorporated
inst.	instant (the present month)
IOU	I owe you
LCL	less than a carload lot
LLC	limited liability company
Ltd.	Limited (stockholders' liability limited to size of their investment)
Ltée	Limitée (French for limited liability)
max.	maximum
mdse.	merchandise
mfr.	manufacturer
min.	minimum
MIS	management information systems
misc.	miscellaneous
mo.	month
NAFTA	North American Free Trade Agreement
pd.	paid

PLC, plc	public limited company (British equivalent of US corporation)
Pty	proprietary
qty.	quantity
R&D	research and development
RE, Re, re	regarding, concerning
recd., rec'd	received
rept.	report or receipt
RSVP	please reply
S.A.	sociedad anónima/société anonyme (Spanish & French for anonymous society, like limited liability)
SOP	standard operating procedure
Spa, SpA	Società per Azione (Italian for corporation)
Srl	Società a responsabilità limitata (Italian for limited responsibility, like limited liability)
treas.	treasurer
VP	vice president
whsle.	wholesale

Business Symbols (used in correspondence and tables)

@	at (for example, 6 copies @ $25.95 each)
&	and (usually used only in company names)
%	percent (out of 100)
$	dollar(s)
¢	cent(s)
£	British pound
¥	Japanese yen
°	degree(s) (temperature or angle)
=	is equal to

≠	is not equal to
#	number (before a numeral — #10)
#	weight in pounds (after a numeral — 10#)
'	feet (6' tall)
"	inches (6'2" tall)
"	ditto (exactly equal; the same)
¶	paragraph
§	section
x	by (11" x 14"); multiplied by (3x5)

Email Abbreviations

By definition these are more likely to turn up in email than on websites. But you should be familiar with some of these abbreviations if only because they may turn up in the email that your site inspires. Many expressions have also turned up in text messaging.

404	I have no idea
AAMOF	as a matter of fact
AFAIK	as far as I know
ATSL	along the same line
B4	before
BBIAB	be back in a bit
BF	boyfriend
BFD	big XXX deal
BRB	be right back
BTW	by the way
CUL8R	see you later
F2F	face to face
FAQ	frequently asked questions
FWIW	for what it's worth
FYI	for your information

G, <G>	grin (placed after a joke or a remark intended as such)
GD&R	grinning, ducking, and running (after a humorously intended insult)
GD&R, vvf	grinning, ducking, and running, very very fast
GIGO	garbage in, garbage out
IANAL	I am not a lawyer (but ...)
IIRC	if I recall correctly
IMHO	in my humble opinion
IMNSHO	in my not so humble opinion
IMO	in my opinion
IOW	in other words
K	OK/okay
LMAO	laughing my ass off
LOL	laughing out loud
OIC	oh, I see
OTOH	on the other hand
PEBCAK	problem exists between chair and keyboard (that is, the user is making a mistake)
PITA	pain in the ass
ROTFL	rolling on the floor laughing
RTFM	read the XXX manual
SUP	what's up?
SYSOP	system operator (manager of a bulletin board or online forum)
TIA	thanks in advance
TIC	tongue in cheek
TTFN	ta-ta for now
TTYL	talk to you later
VBG	very big grin
WRT	with regard to

WYSIWYG	what you see is what you get
YMMV	your mileage may vary

Greek and Latin

A.D.	*Anno Domini*	Year of our Lord
a.m., A.M.	*ante meridiem*	before noon
anon.	*anonymous*	nameless
c. or ca.	*circa*	about (a date)
cf.	*confer*	compare
e.g.	*exempli gratia*	for example
et al.	*et alii*	and other persons
etc.	*et cetera*	and others, and so on
et seq.	*et sequens*	and the following
fl.	*floruit*	flourished
ib., ibid.	*ibidem*	in the same place
i.e.	*id est*	that is
lb.	*libra*	pound
loc. cit.	*loco citato*	in the place cited
n.b.	*nota bene*	note well
ob.	*obiit*	died
op.	*opus*	work
op. cit.	*opere citato*	in the work cited
PhD	*Philosophiae Doctor*	Doctor of Philosophy
p.m., P.M.	*post meridiem*	afternoon
pro tem	*pro tempore*	temporarily
P.S.	*post scriptum*	written afterward
pseud.	*pseudonym*	false name
Q.E.D.	*quod erat demonstrandum*	which was to be demonstrated

q.v.	*quod vide*	which see
R.I.P.	*requiescat in pace*	rest in peace
v.	*vide*	see
viz.	*videlicet*	namely
v., vs.	*versus*	against

Scholarly/General Abbreviations

Note that most lowercase and "mixed" abbreviations take periods. Mixed abbreviations that begin and end with a capital letter don't take periods.

AA	associate in arts (two-year degree)
AS	associate in science (two-year degree)
BA, AB	bachelor of arts
BBA	bachelor of business administration
B.Comm.	bachelor of commerce
BS, B.Sc.	bachelor of sciences
bbl.	barrel(s)
BTU	British Thermal Unit (heat required to raise temperature of 1 pound of water by 1 degree Fahrenheit)
C.	Celsius, Centigrade
c., ©	copyright
DA	doctor of arts
DBA	doctor of business administration
DD	doctor of divinity
DDS	doctor of dental surgery/dental science
cwt.	hundredweight (100 pounds)
deg.	degree, degrees
doz.	dozen
ed.	editor, edited

EdD	doctor of education
est.	estimated
f., ff.	and the following (pages)
hp	horsepower
JD	doctor of jurisprudence
JM	master of jurisprudence
Jr.	junior (the son of someone with the same name)
JSD	doctor of the science of laws
ll.	lines
LLB	bachelor of laws
MA	master of arts
MBA	master of business administration
MD	doctor of medicine
MS, M.Sc.	master of science
MS, ms., mss.	manuscript(s)
n.d.	no date given
NGO	nongovernmental organization
No., no.	numero (number)
n.p.	no numbered pages
obs.	obsolete
p., pp.	page(s)
P.Eng.	professional engineer
PhD	doctor of philosophy
quango	quasi-autonomous nongovernmental organization
SJ	Society of Jesus
ThD	doctor of theology
vol.	volume

APPENDIX

3

UNITS OF MEASUREMENT

Imperial/Traditional Units of Measurement

Traditional units can be confusing, especially to international readers. A Canadian gallon, for example, is larger than an American gallon. If you must use traditional measurement units, try to be consistent; where your readers might need metric equivalents, be sure to supply them. Also, try to avoid mixing metric and traditional units. In Canada, where metric hasn't been fully adopted, people tend to write: I paid $1.25 cents a liter for gas, and my car gets only 15 miles per gallon.

Here is a table of some common traditional units of measurement and their metric equivalents. Note that traditional-unit abbreviations usually take periods, while metric abbreviations do not.

Name/Abbreviation	Metric Equivalent
1 pound/lb.	454 g
1 ounce/oz.	28 g
1 US ton/ton	907 kg
1 imperial ton/ton	1016 kg
1 inch/in.	2.5 cm
1 foot/ft.	0.3 m
1 mile/mi.	1.6 km
1 square foot/sq. ft.	0.09 m²
1 yard/yd.	0.91 m
1 acre/a./ac.	4047 m²
1 acre/a./ac.	0.40 ha (hectares)
1 cubic foot/ft.	0.03 m³
1 US gallon/gal.	3.78 L
1 imperial gallon/gal.	4.54 L
50 degrees Fahrenheit/°F	10°C

SI Numerals

When using SI terms in technical material, use a combination of numerals and abbreviations: 1.6 km, NOT 1.6 kilometers. In other material, use numerals with spelled-out units: Drive 10 kilometers south from the bridge and follow the signs to the vineyard. Do NOT use spelled-out numbers with SI abbreviations (ten km).

In SI usage, a space replaces the comma in numbers with five or more digits:

50 000 votes

$145 000

The space is optional with four digits:

1 152 votes

1152 votes

If four- and five-digit numbers are mixed, all should have a space:

Our opponents spent $9 000 while we spent $10 500.

SI measurements include some units that aren't really SI, including time. What follows is a list of measurements and their abbreviations, which you should present consistently.

Name	Symbol	Quantity
ampere	A	electric current
bel	B	sound intensity
coulomb	C	electric charge
degree Celsius	°C	temperature
hectare	ha	area (100 square meters)
hertz	Hz	frequency
Kelvin	K	temperature
kilogram	kg	weight (2.2 pounds)
knot	kn	1,852 meters per hour
liter	L	volume
meter	m	length
minute	'	plane angle
minute	min	time
nautical mile	M	1,852 meters (marine distance)
second	"	plane angle
ton (metric ton)	t	1,000 kg (2,200 pounds)

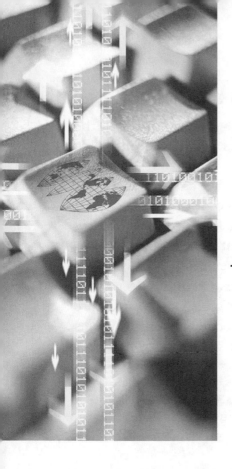

APPENDIX

4

HYPERTEXT STYLE
By Gareth Rees

For several years, Web design pioneer Gareth Rees maintained a very helpful Hypertext Style Guide web page. He has removed it, but has kindly given me permission to reproduce it here, slightly abridged. While written for the Web of the 1990s, it remains relevant.

This material is intended to supplement the CERN Style Guide, www.w3.org/Provider/Style/Overview.html, not to replace it. Some of it is appropriate to people with big databases of material to organize; other bits are directed at people with lame home pages.

Present Coherent Articles as a Whole

Readers understand coherent articles — they see them all the time in magazines, newspapers, journals, and conference proceedings. They don't have much experience of reading articles that have been chopped into pieces — and just as importantly, neither do you. If you choose to present your information in a form close to existing forms, then you know what is successful in that form and what isn't. If you choose to adopt a new form, then you had better think very carefully about exactly how to structure your text for best effect. Read the literature on hypertext for a discussion of how to structure documents for readability; test your documents on readers as though they were computer programs with strange new user interfaces (which, in a sense, they are).

In most browsers, it's easier to navigate within a page than between pages. Dividing a single text into a number of pages, or chunks, means your readers will have to issue a lot of navigational commands to read it.

If you chop your material into small chunks, then readers are prevented from following the thread of your argument because of the long wait for each paragraph to download. If your material is presented as one long, scrolling page, then the initial wait is longer, but once the article has been downloaded the reader can give it his or her full attention.

If you have space, the best solution may be to take advantage of the medium of hypertext and present your article in both ways (as a single complete article and as a multiplicity of paragraphs) and let the reader choose, depending on his or her preference.

Make Sure Deep Structure Is Accessible

In a deep hypertext structure, with indexes at several levels, it is possible for information to be "lost" in the sense that a reader reading the top-level index will be unaware of the existence of deeper information.

This is most likely to happen if different levels of indexes organize information according to different criteria. For example, suppose that a hypothetical university information server has a home page that indexes the home pages of the departments in that university, but doesn't say what information those departments provide. In such a case, the reader must guess which department has the information you need before you can find it.

It is therefore important to provide clues at each level indicating what is to be found on each of the branches. Hierarchical subject trees are examples where this works, because the choices at each level provide access to subsets of the subjects named at the level above. Having a clear index structure also helps you to give an impression of the size of your database.

A good way to prevent your readers getting "lost in hyperspace" (a common feeling when browsing a complex structure) is to give them plenty of clues as to how big your database is.

The best clue you can provide is a complete listing of entries (even if such a list isn't appropriate on the home page, it can be provided separately). A top-level index of categories should annotate each entry with the number of documents to be found by following that entry. If you can find an appropriate visual organizing principle, then a graphical overview might help those of your readers with fast connections and graphical browsers. To give a correct impression of the size of your database, you need to distinguish internal and external links.

Some home pages freely mix links pointing to documents in the database at that site with documents stored elsewhere, as though the Web were a single amorphous information resource. But amorphous doesn't necessarily imply useful.

If you maintain a personal home page, then —

(a) **Don't use links as footnotes.** Footnotes distract from a line of argument; if the material in a footnote can't be integrated into the body of the text, it probably doesn't belong in a footnote either. Just because you can include jottings, notes, side issues, and other material in a hypertext document, doesn't mean you have to.

(b) **Annotate your references.** Please, annotate your lists. Try to provide a short description of the contents of the destination of the link (but use your discretion; some titles are self-explanatory, and a blurb that says nothing useful is as bad as no blurb at all). Think of it as your way of adding value to the list; anyone can compile a list of links (the Web-crawling robots have databases with hundreds of thousands of URLs), but you have to read and understand the documents in order to write useful descriptions and thus make your list a valuable resource.

(c) **Don't discuss your own pages.** The mere lack of anything to say doesn't stop some people; instead of writing about the world "out there," they discuss their own web pages — how they were written, when they were written, what's new about them, what their friends had to say about them, what the usage statistics are, who's read them, and so on.

APPENDIX

5

EXERCISE KEY

Exercise 1: Converting Prose to Bullets

The key conventions of modern science fiction:

- Isolated society (island, lost valley, planet)
- Morally significant language (Orwell's Newspeak)
- Important documents (Book of Bokonon in Vonnegut's *Cat's Cradle*)
- Ideological attitude toward sex (Huxley's *Brave New World*)
- An inquisitive outsider (Genly Ai in Le Guin's *The Left Hand of Darkness*)

Exercise 2: Activating the Passive

Here are active-voice versions of the passive-voice sentences. Other versions could be equally acceptable.

1. Some researchers argue that the US Air Force retrieved alien bodies from a crashed spacecraft near Roswell, New Mexico, in 1947.

2. Critics hailed Miles Davis's *Sketches of Spain* as one of his finest works.

3. Researchers at Xerox originally developed graphical user interface.

4. A local physician stopped a 19th-century outbreak of cholera in London by removing the handle from a neighborhood water pump.

5. We carefully chose these graphics to illustrate each step of the process.

Exercise 3: Using Anglo-Saxon Vocabulary

1. altercation: angry dispute

2. antagonist: adversary, opponent

3. capitulate: give up, surrender

4. celestial: pertaining to the sky or heavens

5. demotic: common, popular

6. epitome: typical (or extreme) example; concise summary

7. fiduciary: acting as trustee or guardian; held in trust

8. gravamen: most serious part of an accusation; essential part or gist

9. impediment: obstacle, handicap

10. litigious: quarrelsome, quick to go to court

GLOSSARY

This book uses many terms that have become standard in web-writing but may be baffling to "newbies" — newcomers to the world of the Internet. Here are brief definitions of some of the terms people have the most trouble with:

archive (verb): to store a document on a website, usually the full text of something originally written for print on paper. The document is not likely to be changed or updated.

blog (noun or verb): from the term *web log*, meaning a website that is frequently updated with information, usually about a particular subject. To blog is to post information to such a site.

blurb (noun): a short description of what readers can expect if they follow a certain link to another page.

browser (noun): a software program (such as Internet Explorer or Firefox) that can find and display the files on a website. In effect, the browser copies the files temporarily onto your computer. It will also let you download permanent copies of the site's text, graphics, and other elements.

chunk (verb or noun): create short passages of text that can be displayed on a single screen. Chunking can entail breaking up longer text into independent segments, or writing brief passages from scratch. A chunk of text is usually no more than 100 words long, and may be much shorter.

cookie (noun): a piece of information that a website can install on your computer. When you return to that site, it will recognize you from your cookie and may display the site as you requested on your last visit.

download (verb): copy a file from a website onto your computer. This may be a text file, a graphic, or a whole software application.

email (verb or noun): electronic mail — messages sent over the Internet. Such messages may include copies of earlier messages. Many websites include email addresses enabling readers to send messages to the site's creator or persons connected to it in some way. As a verb: "I'll email the changes to you this afternoon." The spelling "e-mail" is also correct.

e-zine (noun): a website in the form of an electronic magazine, including articles, pictures, video, audio, and other effects. An e-zine may be the creation of a single person or of many contributors. Some are paying markets for freelance writers.

FAQs (noun): frequently asked questions. Pronounced "facks." A list of questions and answers on a given topic, often included on a website to save its creator from tediously repeating the same answers.

flame (verb): send insulting and abusive messages by email, often in response to a real or perceived insult or abuse.

front page (noun): the introductory page of a website, often containing introductory comments (orientation), a table of contents (information), and a set of links to other pages on the site (action).

hit-and-run (adjective): used to describe both a method of information retrieval — scanning and moving on to another item — and the kind of item most easily scanned. This is usually a single chunk of text, visible on a single screen without the need to scroll down.

home page (noun): synonym for *front page*, but also used to mean a whole website with more information about its topic than any other such site. Your personal page is your "home page," for example, but your page celebrating Holly Cole may not be *her* home page.

hook (noun): an unusual statement or graphic that draws and holds attention so that users will read an entire file or explore a major part of the site.

HTML (noun): hypertext markup language, a simple code that turns text and graphics into something that a Web browser can display.

hypertext (noun): an electronic file containing a document (or part of a document) with electronic links to other documents. A hypertext may exist on a CD-ROM, such as one for an encyclopedia; as a "help" file in a software application; or on a website. A single graphic, if it contains links to other graphics or a text file, is also hypertext. The term *hypertext* applies both to an individual file with its links, and to all the other files it links to.

Internet (noun): the group of networks permitting access to computers (and their contents) around the world. Usually capitalized when referring to the global network, and written in lowercase when referring to a smaller network.

intranet (noun): a network of computers accessible only to members of an organization, such as a company or school.

jolt (noun): a sensory or intellectual stimulus created or transmitted by computer — for example, a sound file that announces, "You've got mail," or an animated image, or an emotionally charged email message.

keyword (noun): a word or phrase used to help identify a file that may be of interest. "Spaghetti alla primavera" could be a keyword in a search for Italian recipes; "Web style" could be a keyword in a search for advice on writing text for websites.

link (noun or verb): a word, phrase, or graphic on a website that contains a code with the address of another electronic file. Clicking the cursor on a link commands the browser to seek that address and to display its content. Also, to create or provide such an address: "This page also links to other sites offering advice on Italian cooking."

listserv (noun): an electronic discussion group focused on a particular topic. Everyone belonging to the listserv receives messages posted from other members to the listserv, and can see messages to all other members. Members must subscribe to listservs if they wish to post their own comments.

meta tag (noun): an invisible word or phrase that provides a keyword, usually located at the top of a web page's coding. Search engines sometimes list pages by the number of times they find the keyword; a site with an invisible meta tag that says "primavera primavera primavera" will turn up sooner than a site that just says "Spaghetti alla primavera." Some search engines, however, are programmed to reject such repetitive meta tags. The purpose of the meta tag is to attract more visits (or "hits") so the website can charge more to advertisers, or attract more paying subscribers.

navigation bar (noun): a part of the site, usually visible on every page, that permits movement among various pages as well as movement to pages on other sites.

navigation button (noun): an image or text that provides a link to another part of the site — for example, to the home page or an archives page.

online (adjective or adverb): referring to the Internet or the World Wide Web. "She reviewed several online documents" (documents stored in a computer linked to the Web). "He researched online for several hours" (went from one site to another looking for information). Can also refer to materials stored on a CD-ROM or DVD, or as part of a software application, as in "Online Help."

PDF (noun): Portable Document Format. A way of storing and displaying files so that, using the Adobe Acrobat reader (a free software application), the files appear with all their original formatting, fonts, graphics, and other details — including internal hypertext links and links to other sites.

plug-in (noun): a software extension that "plugs in" to your browser so you can see or hear some special aspect of a website. RealAudio, for example, lets you hear an audio file that it can download.

resolution (noun): the fineness of detail available on a computer screen; a high-resolution screen provides a sharper, clearer image than a low-resolution screen.

scrolling (verb or adjective): moving a long text file up or down the computer screen. Many readers dislike scrolling. Some long, scrolling texts contain internal links that enable readers to go straight to the section of interest.

search engine (noun): a program that rapidly searches millions of websites for the word or phrase you have specified. The engine will then display links to all the sites it has found, with the likeliest or most popular pages first. Google is by far the dominant search engine, but many search engines specialize in particular topics such as medicine or engineering.

splash page (noun): an introductory page, often with a dramatic graphic including video and audio. The user must click on it to reach the real front page of the website.

stack (verb or noun): to connect two or more chunks of website text with a link. If your recipe for "spaghetti alla primavera" includes a link to a recipe for "spaghetti trastevere" (another chunk), you have created a stack.

stickiness (noun): the quality of content and display in a website that encourages visitors to "stick around" to explore it.

surf (verb): to move from one website to another, especially on impulse.

upload (verb): to send a computer file to another computer elsewhere on the Internet. For example, you may upload a family photo to your blog, which resides on the server of your blog provider.

URL (noun): uniform resource locator. The address of a website. It tells your browser where to look for a particular page. In many cases the browser will assume it's a commercial site if you simply type in the company name. If you type in "Microsoft," for example, your browser will automatically seek out www.microsoft.com and open the home page of the Microsoft Corporation.

webmaster (noun): the person responsible for maintaining a website. The webmaster may also create the site or may allow others to create and upload pages to the site.

web page (noun): a single electronic file displaying text, graphics, or sound through a browser online, usually linked to at least one other page.

website (noun): a number of pages linked to one another and usually dealing with closely related topics; a website is usually located on a single "server" (networked computer).

The following components are included on the CD-ROM for use on a Windows-based PC. Mac users can go to Writing for the Web at http://crofsblog.typepad.com to download these files.

Exercises

1. Converting Prose to Bullets
2. Activating the Passive
3. Using Anglo-Saxon Vocabulary
4. Analyzing Corporate Websites
5. Editing Text for Websites (4 exercises)

PowerPoint Slide Show

- Introduction to Webwriting (in PowerPoint and PDF formats)

Useful Links

- URLs from and relating to the book, including the author's blogs

Glossary